Title: **Archery. A walk through its history**
Author: **Jorge J. López Bordón**
Illustrations: **Javier Ortega de Vicente**

Layout and printing
Dadú Estudio
Batalla del Salado, 14
28045 Madrid
Tel. 913 854 315

Copyright: Jorge J. López Bordón
ISBN: 9798842720118

First edition: November of 2021

All rights reserved. The content of this work is protected by law. Reproduction in whole or partial in any format without permission of the author is prohibited.

ARCHERY

A WALK THROUGH ITS HISTORY

JORGE J. LÓPEZ BORDÓN

I dedicate this book to Pino Gopar,
the woman who has always been by my side in good times
and bad, and who encouraged me throughout this project.

CONTENTS

I.	The bow in pre-history	11
II.	The bow in the Ancient Age	17
	2.1 Sumerian civilization	17
	2.2 Akkadian Empire	21
	2.3 Egyptian civilization	23
	2.4 Assyrian civilization	28
	2.5 Persian civilization	31
	2.6 Scythian people	34
	2.7 Greek civilization	37
	2.8 Roman civilization	42
	2.9 Hunnic Empire	45
III.	The Middle Ages	49
	3.1 Europe in the Middle Ages	51
	3.1.1 The bow in medieval wars	52
	3.1.2 England and the longbow	63
	3.1.3 The Normans	69
	3.2 Spain, islam and the Arab bow	69
IV.	The bow in the Asian continent	85
	4.1 The Magyar bow	86
	4.2 The Mongolian bow	89
	4.3 The Chinese bow	98
	4.4 The Japanese bow	102
	4.5 Other Asian towns	113
	4.5.1 The bow in Korea	113
	4.5.2 The bow in Vietnam	115
	4.5 3 The bow in Tíbet	117
	4.5.4 The bow in Bhutan	120
	4.5.5 The bow in Northern Asia and Siberia	122

V. The bow in the American continent 123
    5.1 The bow and arrow in pre-columbian America 124
        5.1.1 Central American people 126
        5.1.2 The bow and arrow in South America 132
        5.1.3 The bow and arrow in North America 143

VI. The bow in the Modern and Contemporary Ages 151
    6.1 Women and the «renaissance» of archery 152
    6.2 The bow in the 20th century: two world wars, the interwar period and the Olympic Games 157
        6.2.1 Archery in Paralympic Games 161
    6.3 Archery as a recreational sport 162
        6.3.1 Target archery 163
        6.3.2 Field archery 164
        6.3.3 2D and 3D animal archery 165
        6.3.4 Clout archery 170
        6.3.5 Flight archery 171
        6.3.6 Ski archery 171
    6.4 Archery nowadays 172
        6.4.1 Bowfishing 172
        6.4.2 Field hunting 175

VII. The bow and arrow: humanism and science 181
    7.1 The bow: a mythological tool 182
        7.1.1 Cupid and Eros: the bow in the Greek and Roman mythology. The origin of Valentine 183
        7.1.2 Archery in universal mythology 187
            7.1.2.1 Greek mythology 187
            7.1.2.2 Nordic mythology 188
            7.1.2.3 Asian mythology 190
    7.2 The bow in Abrahamic religions 194
        7.2.1 Arrows in religious art 196
    7.3 The bow and arrow in science 199
    7.4 The bow and arrow in literature and fiction 201

This great little book is the consequence of a desire and a need: achieving a story capable of immersing us in the history of archery and its many and very different uses over the centuries, influencing traditions and religions since pre-history, where this journey begins, up to the present moment.

Starting from that pre-history, in which the use of the bow and arrow could make the difference between living or dying, we will travel back in time to make an exciting journey that will take us from the Ancient Age to the Modern Age, ending the tour in the Contemporary era, why not, speculating on the future of this exciting activity that, after being relegated to oblivion by firearms, reached the rank of Olympic sport at the 1900 Paris games and was consolidated as such in Munich in 1972.

Do you want to take this trip with me? Let's start!

CHAPTER I

TYE BOW IN PRE-HISTORY

It was the summer of 1879. For the second time, Marcelino Sanz de Sautola, an amateur jurist and archaeologist, visited the Altamira Cave in the Cantabrian town of Santillana del Mar. The cave had been discovered eleven years earlier by a local hunter, Modesto Cubillas Pérez, and Marcelino had visited it for the first time in 1875, without being able to anticipate how different his return would be.

After a visit to the Universal Exhibition in Paris in 1878, Marcelino Sautola had been fascinated by the exhibits on the Stone Age. The objective of returning to Altamira was to explore the cave, in order to find remains of bone and flint.

It is necessary to see this situation in perspective. Archeology has come a long way in the last century, and bone and flint remains are not comparable to great finds, such as the Valley of the Kings in Egypt or Atapuerca. However, Marcelino's wish was almost heresy by that time. At the end of the 19th century, the study of pre-history was still an incipient field of knowledge, and discoveries based on scientific evidence were at least controversial for a society still deeply rooted in rigid religious convictions. But, for Marcelino, this was not an impediment.

Accompanied by his eight-year-old daughter, María, he set out for the cave, which was located inside a farm, where he was a sharecropper. As they walked, Marcelino couldn't help but think about the remains of what appeared to be bones that he had found in 1875, or about the black marks on the cave wall. Upon arrival, the man stood at the mouth of the grotto, a small opening in a hill, but Maria walked down a long, dark corridor to a side room.

—Dad, run! ¡Come and see the animals! —she shouted, excited.

Animals? What animals? It had to be the product of a child's own imagination. At most, there would be a bat. Arriving at the room, Sautola could not believe what her eyes saw. The entire vault was covered by figures in reddish and dark tones that, indeed, looked like animals: horses, bison... anthropomorphic figures. What was all that? How long had those figures been there? Who had painted them? What did they represent? Without knowing it, María Sanz de Sautola y Escalante had discovered what would later be known as the Sistine Chapel of quaternary art.

Altamira and its bison were the first indication of palaeolithic art, but not the last. In 1917, almost three decades after the death of Marcelino Sanz de Sautola, who died in disrepute for his defense of the authenticity of the cave paintings, **Albert Rodá discovered the Caballos Cave in the province of Castellón. There was a mural, dated towards the 7000 a. C., painted on the rock of the cave, and it had a scene from hunting.**

In the scene, a group of men, represented as figures reduced to their basic and essential anatomical features, stand in front of some deer that they are going to shoot. Far from the ritual character of the Altamira paintings, the Caballos Cave showed what life was really like for the first humans. For the first time, we had a real representation of our ancestors as hunters. For the first time, we could visualize the man wielding his flexible wooden bow, watching his hands tighten the string as his eyes focused on the target. We could even imagine how these rudimentary arrows cut through the air at full speed until the sharp, triangular tip entered the victim and killed him.

Cave painting

The Altamira Cave and the Caballos Cave also allow us to observe the progress of our ancestors. The first humans lived in semi-nomadic tribes and fed on carrion and the collection of fruits, leaves and roots. Their basic concerns were getting food and defending themselves from the dangers of their environment. Over time, they also learned the art of hunting, which was able to develop thanks to two factors.

In the first place, and as the paintings in the Caballos Cave show, the man developed new techniques of social organization; however, these would not have been successful if, in addition, there had not been an improvement in hunting instruments.

At first, our ancestors hunted with axes. However, exposure to potential prey brought injuries and death among hunters. Over time, the man invented the spear, but even hunting less dangerous animals was complicated, since the approach movement and the abrupt sequence of movements to launch the projectile used to alert the game to the hunter's position. The man realized that hunters with longer arms managed to launch the projectile at a greater distance without being seen, which considerably increased the success of hunting days.

The ingenuity paid off. Ancient man, who could not match the large mammals and fauna of the time in terms of strength, nor did he have the same speed as the smaller species, managed to match the physical conditions of the animals around him, creating a propellant that gave the spear more speed and power, which allowed it to reach much further and have a better flight.

The first mechanical aid he used was the spear or *atlatl* (dart or stolic spear in Spanish), a kind of launcher or propellant for the spear, primitive and light, similar to the one used today by the Australian aborigines. The *atlatl* was composed of a wooden shaft with a slit in which the spear, made of deer antler, was placed. Later, feathering was added to stabilize the rear, similar to that of the arrows. The man held it from the front, and as the weapon was thrown, the launcher became an extension of the arm, transferring more energy and acceleration to the projectile.

Due to the degradation of the wood, loose stone points are usually unearthed; however, the term *assagaya* or *atlatl* refers both to the point found and to the entire object.

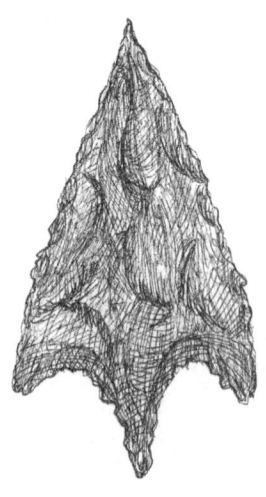

Flint tip

It should be noted that the different civilizations did not evolve in the same way throughout pre-history. Thus, the bow and its use appeared in different parts of the planet at different times. In fact, today there are still tribes technologically anchored in pre-history in areas such as Africa or the Amazon.

Early settlers in the Americas also replaced hand-thrown javelins with propellants. Its widespread use accelerated the extinction of the great American cenozoic mammals, something that would also happen on the Australian continent. The *atlatl* was gradually replaced by the bow, a much more effective tool, but more complex to use and make. In addition to the bow, some pre-columbian cultures also used other weapons, such as slingshots and blowguns.

The Aztec indians used propellants for darts that were the same size or smaller than an arrow, but just as effective. At first, they were a piece of wood folded and tied at both ends by a piece of gut. It was a simple but useful weapon for shooting at a greater distance than a spear, even with the help of a launcher. Over time would come the invention of the bow. Upon arriving in the New World, Cortés and the conquerors verified –sometimes firsthand– the effectiveness of the weapon that was still used by the indigenous people of South America.

In Australia, the propellant used by the aborigines was known as the woomera. The first settlers of Australia, Tasmania and the surrounding islands arrived around 50 000 B.C. They were semi-nomadic people, dedicated to the collection and hunting of marsupials, monotremes and other unique native species, some of them even deadly for humans, as a result of the separation of Antarctica, about 30 million years ago, and the isolation of Australia and its islands.

Although the Australian aborigines never developed the bow and arrow, this did not prevent them from being excellent hunters. In fact, it is suspected that, in addition to climate change and the subsequent introduction of indigenous species, the aboriginal dominance of spears and boomerangs was responsible for the extinction of part of Australia's megafauna.

The oldest bow in the world found so far belongs to the neolithic. It was found at the site of La Draga, in Gerona, and it is estimated that it was made around 5400-5200 B.C. It is about 108 centime-

ters long and it is made of yew wood, known for its resistance and for the growth time of the tree, a protected species in Catalonia today.

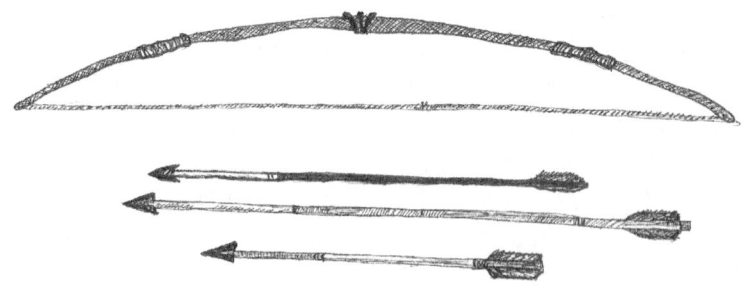

Pre-historic bow and arrow set

Until the arrival of the Bronze Age in the Mediterranean area, around the year 3500 B.C., no major changes were seen in terms of weapons, but there was a gradual improvement of the existing one.

CHAPTER II

THE BOW IN THE ANCIENT AGE

The bow was already mentioned in the biblical scriptures and in the Old Testament and, over the centuries, it evolved to become a weapon that served both for hunting as for war, becoming an object of everyday life. The simple bow gave way to the compound bow, which would later spread from Mesopotamia to the entire Orient, the Asian steppes, and Eastern Europe.

This second chapter of the book explores the evolution of the bow and arrow during the Ancient Age, from 4000 to 3000 B.C. approximately, until the 5th century, after the fall of the western Roman Empire. To illustrate this story, we will focus on the people who populated the Eurasian block and who were the cradle of civilization: Sumerians, Akkadians, Egyptians, Romans, Greeks, Huns, Scythians and Persians.

2.1 Sumerian civilization

One day of November, in 1872, a young man named George Smith ran out of one of the back rooms of the British Museum, excited and undressing. It is not known for sure if it was joy that led him to undress, or a temporary attack of madness, but the reason for his joy has survived to this day: he had managed to decipher what is considered to be the greatest, oldest epic poem ever known, written about 4000-3500 years before our era in ancient Mesopotamia.

> He who managed to see the deep
> He who was wise in all respects
> Gilgamesh
> who saw the deep
> He who was wise in affairs everywhere
> and he learned of all things the sum of wisdom
> He saw what was secret
> and he discovered what was hidden
> He brought back from him a story
> from times before the flood
> He embarked on a long journey
> reaching the point of being exhausted
> he found peace
> and he wrote all his work on a stone
> tablet.

Thus begins the epic poem that tells how Gilgamesh, –two-thirds God– has to face his human side, his mistakes and failures, and even something as inevitable as death. The work was later known for being the first to mention the great flood and the tower of Babel, even before the Bible. But the epopeya has a much deeper moral. Gilgamesh's fight against death leads him to realize that the only immortality one can aspire to is that which comes from leaving behind a lasting achievement.

Ancient Mesopotamia and the Sumerian civilization are the first examples of this human aspect of eternity. We owe the Sumerians their inventions –including beer, grown from barley, the twelve-month calendar in use today, and the clock–, the construction of the first cities and, most important, writing. It was them, the oldest civilization known to date, who took the first steps towards the development of humanity as we know it. Even today, although a large part of this heritage has been destroyed through successive wars, archaeological work has continued to uncover spectacular reliefs, sculptures and tablets with cuneiform writing, discoveries that help us to find out how we have come this far.

Archaeological sites have shown that the Sumerians were great warriors. Just look at the type of cities they built: walled, high-walled, double-walled, built with strong materials, indicating that the kings who ruled the city-states had to face sieges.

An example is the city of Mari, which had two lines of walls. The first, a sloping dam that protected the city from the floods of the Euphrates River, was built coinciding with the founding of the city, around 2900 B.C. However, as the discoveries of cities II and III of Mari show, this outer dike became a defensive wall over time. There were about 350 meters between the two lines of defense, an arrangement similar to that later adopted by medieval castles with their walls and moats. Even so, these mechanisms did not prevent the city of Mari from being destroyed twice, once by King Naram-Sin of Akkad, in 2238 B.C., and another by Hammurapi of Babylon, around the year 1760 B.C. And the fact is that, although the distance between the two defensive walls might seem sufficient to protect the cities from technical and technological advances at a military level, the Sumerians were also the first civilization to have a professional army, which, although it allowed them to protect themselves from neighboring people, not so militarily developed, plunged them into some 2000 years of almost constant wars between different city-states.

The first recorded Sumerian war took place between the forces of Lagash and Umma in about 2525 B.C. Cuneiform tablets record how the king of the city of Lagash led an army made up mostly of foot soldiers, specialized in hand-to-hand battle. The weapons of this infantry corps were spears, helmets made of copper, and leather or wicker shields. The lancers were arranged in what is now known as a phalanx formation, a single row of fighters very close to each other and with a depth of between 8 and 16 warriors; this extremely poor strategic position gave them great disadvantages against foreign invaders.

The first of the great inventions that gave the Sumerians a certain military advantage was the chariot. Although the original floats were clumsy and slow, little by little they could be improved and incorporated into the realm of warfare. Four onagers pulled a cage made of three-piece wheeled, interwoven baskets. Two people moved in these carts who, in addition, transported war material, including spears and shields.

As military technology developed, spears were replaced by simple bows, made from a single piece of wood. Some studies and analyzes have revealed that they were made of various materials, including wood, horn, bone, tendons or ligaments.

Representation of a Sumerian with his bow

The real revolution, however, was the discovery of bronze around 2800 B.C. and its incorporation into the technology of the time. **The armies of ancient Mesopotamia developed the compound bow, an efficient innovation compared to the simple bow that, by revolutionizing military tactics, allowed the expansion of another Sumerian people, the Akkadians.** The compound bow, contrary to the simple bows made in a single body and in a single material, such as wood, was composed (its body, blades and handle) by a succession of blades of different materials.

Traditionally these sheets were alternately glued one on top of the other forming three layers. The central sheet is usually made of wood (in Europe and Mesopotamia) or bamboo (in the Far East); the inner sheet of the bow, the one facing the archer, is made of bone or antler; and the outer sheet is made of tendons.

The compound bow originated with the intention of overcoming the limitations presented by the simple bow, since it offered several advantages, such as a greater reach, lighter weight, smaller size and easier and smoother opening.

The maximum draw of a bow is referenced to the length of the archer's arm. Compound bows had the tips of the limbs curved forward when they were drawn, thanks to their previous curvature, which allowed energy to be stored without the archer having opened an inch, in contrast to the simple bow, which, being rectum, had no previous energy. This small modification in the design of the bows was a revolution for the time.

However, the compound bow had some disadvantages, since it needed more maintenance and was more sensitive to humidity. In addition, its assembly required considerable strength and two people were needed to perform the task. These were rudimentary bows, if we look at them from the 21st century –where materials such as wood, carbon fiber or glass are used–, but they were very modern for the time.

2.2 Akkadian Empire

Around the year 2300 B.C., the Syrian Sumerians were invaded by the Akkadians, people who had dominated the region since 2550 B.C. King Sargon I expanded north, conquering all of Mesopotamia, and established the capital at Acad, also called Acadia or Agade, the actual location which is still unknown.

Thanks to the works of writers and sculptors, these ancient conquests have come down to our time and we can learn more about how the wars that took place during this period, as well as the tactics used; but, above all, we can observe the evolution of weapons, more specifically, the bow and arrow.

In these works, you can see the representation of dignitaries carrying bows and arrows, and some of them have a recurve bow and an arrow in their hands. Findings like these have allowed us to study and value this unmistakable shape of the recurve bow.

As for the offensive material, **the Akkadians used compound bows, which had far more power and range than spears and even the older bows, which were made from a single piece of wood and were more difficult to handle. The use of this type of bow by the Akkadians was an early sign of progress,** since, although it is known that metals such as tin were used in Mesopotamia, including present-day Syria, **there is no archaeological evidence that proves that the compound bow was part of the Sumerian army.**

From modern experiments carried out with replicas of Egyptian compound bows, we know that the speed reached by the arrows was 50 meters per second, so their penetration capacity was quite considerable. Moreover, **this type of bow allowed different types of arrows to be shot, from light ones, capable of reaching long distances, to heavier bronze arrows, which could pierce shields and other body protection at close range. The compound bow revolutionized military techniques.** This was demonstrated in 1971 by the French protestant archaeologist and theologian André Parrot, who published a representation attributed to the Ancient Dynastic Period III of Mesopotamia (2600 B.C. - 2334 B.C.) that shed new light on the use of the compound bow, especially regarding to the art of the siege, and how the Akkadians succeeded in establishing the first real empire in ancient Mesopotamia.

The new invention allowed, mainly, to develop tactics that had a devastating effect on a psychological level for the besieged. An archer of the time was capable of launching around ten arrows per minute at a distance of up to 40 meters. The arrows, in addition, could be poisoned or set on fire. In the latter case, very powerful bows were not used to avoid extinguishing the arrows, and hundreds of them fell on the enemy from a height of about 30 meters. Is it possible to imagine the terror of those soldiers, receiving a rain of fire coming from the sky, as if sent by an accursed god?

With the incorporation of bronze weapons, personal protection systems were developed to counteract the damage of the new weapons. It can be said that it was the first arms race in history. However, all this development did not prevent that in 2150 B.C. the Gutu (also called Guti) arrived from territories east of the Tigris and destabilized the Akkadian Empire.

Although their arrival allowed a restructuring of hegemonies in the area, internal rebellions and invasions of nomadic people weakened the Sumerians to the point that, in 2000 B.C., the arrival of the Amorites, people of Semitic origin from the Arabian desert, marked the end of the Sumerian civilization. The Amorites came to dominate the entire area and built what would later become the Babylonian Empire.

The legacy of the Sumerian civilization, its inventions and discoveries have lasted to this day. But we are not the only ones: there were also contemporary people and civilizations that were influenced by their relations with populations of ancient Mesopotamia. One of the clearest examples is the Egyptian civilization, whose script has deep-seated parallels with the cuneiform script. In addition, as we will see below, the benefits of Egypt-Mesopotamia relations, which are believed to have begun in the 4th century B.C., led to many more advances.

2.3 Egyptian civilization

«At first I couldn't see anything, only how the hot air coming out of the chamber caused the candle flame to flicker. But, as my eyes adjusted to the light, the details in the chamber began to take shape in the dust: strange animals, statues, and gold –the gleam of gold– everywhere».

ARCHERY

This paragraph corresponds to an entry in the diary of Howard Carter, a name that may not sound familiar to profane Egyptologists, but it was him who discovered what is to date the best preserved tomb in ancient Egypt, that of Pharaoh Tutankhamun. This tomb is famous for the curse that is said to have fallen on all those who participated in its discovery.

After 30 years in Egypt unearthing tombs, Carter had secured funding from the English aristocrat Lord Carnarvon for his expedition into the Valley of the Kings, on the banks of the Nile, to find the tomb of the boy-king. However, the operation was not having the expected success. So much so that Carnarvon had threatened to cut funding the following year if there were no results.

On November 4th of 1922, Carter's luck changed. His water bearer stumbled over what might have seemed like a simple stone to someone inexperienced, a stone that was nothing more than an entrance step to a burial place. A year later Carter and his employees entered the main chamber of the tomb. There they found gold reliquaries, chests of jewels, alabaster statuettes... all around an impressive stone sarcophagus, which, in turn, contained three other sarcophagi. The last and smallest, made of pure gold, contained a mummy that had been preserved for 3000 years. It was Tutankhamun, King Tut, the king who was enthroned when he was just a 9 or 10-year-old boy.

Among the possessions with which the boy-king had been buried were twenty-four bows that he had possibly used during his life. Seventeen of those bows were made of wood in one piece, and the remaining seven were of a markedly different design: they were compound bows with angulations at their ends. Although it seems irrelevant, this discovery has allowed us to better understand the origin and use of the bow and arrow in ancient Egypt.

Various paintings show hunters and warriors using a bow, indicating that the bow and arrow are as old as Egyptian civilization. It is known that the early pharaohs were fond of hunting with a bow, and also used it as a weapon of war.

It was customary for socially well-positioned individuals to hire mercenaries of Nubian origin, reputed to be excellent archers, and reference to them has even been found in the tomb of Mesehti, high priest in Asjut, during the 11th dynasty. The funerary bed housed a series of wooden figures in two groups of forty soldiers, some were Egyptian spearmen and the other Nubian archers, troops that used to be used as border guards. The images show them as men with black skin, who wear a colored shenti that is attached to the waist by a colorful sash, and with their inseparable bow and arrows. The chronicles assure that they had a great physical resistance and their ability to camouflage was known, they were skirmishers. His shots could have a long range and his arrows could deal a lot of damage. The Nubians' skill with the bow survived the centuries, even defeating an entire Roman army in 20 B.C.

Nubian archer

It can be imagined the advantage that the use of this weapon gave them in the recurring wars with their neighbors, especially when they counterattacked with much more rudimentary weapons, such as spears and slings.

The Egyptians were pioneers in using the bow as a weapon of war, around the year 3500 B.C. The first bows were monolithic or simple, had a single curvature and were composed of a single relatively large piece of wood. The rope, in turn, was made of vegetable fiber tendons or ropes. This type of bow, harder and more expensive to use –because it does not take effort from the archer–, was used during the early days of the Egyptian Empire.

Contact with neighbors in the Near East, especially the Hyksos, brought about the gradual arrival of the compound bow to the land of the pharaohs. Although the compound bow began to be used in Egypt around 1700 B.C., the simple bow continued to be used during the dynasties of Thutmose III (1481- 1425 B.C.) and Amenhotep II (1425 - 1400 B.C.). It is true that, unlike the compound bow, simple bows required less maintenance, were less sensitive to moisture and could be assembled by one person. However, the advantages of the compound bow (greater range, lightness and size, as well as greater ease of opening) outweighed its disadvantages, which led to the inmediate replacement of one by another.

Specifically, the land of the pharaohs saw the birth of a compound bow known as the Egyptian compound bow, made of wood, bone or other resistant materials, while, as a novelty, the strings were made from the intestines of sheep or other animals, which were stretched until the desired bow length was achieved. As already mentioned, the forward curved limbs of the compound bow allowed the archer to store energy and give the bow the maximum draw of his arm. Like contemporary archers, ancient Egyptian archers used tough cloth or leather arm guards, as well as finger guards, as tough as or harder than leather.

At first, the arrowheads were made of flint; flint would give way to bronze in the second millennium B.C., until arrowheads began to be made of iron a millennium later. The leaf-shaped points, used in the predynastic period, were replaced by others that were more pointed and that pierced surfaces more easily.

A WALK THROUGH ITS HISTORY

The characteristics of the Egyptian compound bow are summarized in the following table.

Historical period	2300 - 1400 B.C.
Bow length	62" to 68" (160 to 173 cm).
Stem material	Hard canes and branches.
Arrowheads	Tied to the stem with a natural thread edge. Arrows were feathered with 3" (7,5 cm) long feathers and glued down with shellac.
Arrow length	34" to 37" (86 to 94 cm).
Arrow weight	0,4 – 0,5 oz (10 - 14 gr).

Egyptian painting. Ancient pharaoh mural

The compound bow became the favored weapon of the Egyptian army. In the realm of warfare, they almost perfectly combined a lightweight, easy-to-use compound bow with its use adapted to fast battle tanks that allowed the enemy to be easily surrounded. These chariots were not an Egyptian invention, but an import from other people with whom they had conflicts, such as the Assyrians in Mesopotamia. **What was, indeed, an Egyptian invention were compound bows that offered the possibility of remaining mounted for much longer without becoming deformed or losing power.**

The Egyptian archers were located in the first row of the battle and either on foot or in a chariot, they destroyed the enemy lines with their arrows, thus paving the way for the infantry and cavalry corps, who entered with melee weapons of war (spears, swords, axes, maces, etc.) and protected by a metal breastplate fastened with wide leather straps.

Thanks to these combat tactics, the Egyptian soldiers formed the most feared army of their time, exercising a military supremacy that no other civilization could face, not even the warlike Assyrians. This was all due to a bow, an arrow, and the ability to transform, improve and know how to use them.

2.4 Assyrian civilization

> The word of the Lord came to Jonah son of Amittai: «Go to the great city of Nineveh and preach against it, because its wickedness has come up before me».
>
> (Jonah 1:1-3)

In 1843 the French consul in Mosul (Iraq), the archaeologist and historian Paul-Émile Botta, had the honor of discovering the walled city of Dur Sharrukin[1]. Born around 2600 B.C., starting from the city-state of Aššur, on the banks of the Tigris River, north of ancient Mesopotamia, the Assyrian civilization was the first to be the object of successful

---

1.- In Assyrian, «the Sargon Fortress».

archaeological excavations. Hence, the study of ancient Mesopotamia is known as assyriology.

However, several sources had already testified to the existence of the Assyrian Empire. The Old Testament recorded the relations between the people of Judah and the Assyrians, known for their fame as excellent merchants; and it is also mentioned the city of Nineveh (Iraq today), the place where God sent the prophet Jonah to proclaim His word and prevent its destruction. As a result of these biblical narratives, a negative image of Assyria was created, a brutal and oppressive civilization.

Assyrian archer on horseback

How much truth there is in these biblical prophecies is difficult to know. What archaeological excavations have shown is that the Assyrians were a cultured people. In the mid-nineteenth century, literary works and scientific texts written on tablets[2] were discovered at the sites of Assyrian capitals. In addition, it is known that the scholars of the time, the wise men belonging to the elites of society, had at their disposal collections of texts that could be considered the prelude to the current libraries, such as the collection of Surbanipal, in Nineveh.

The sites have also shown the warlike side of the Assyrians, who were not only in conflict with the ancient Egyptians but also with their Babylonian neighbours. And, in the same way that the Assyrians were much more advanced than other people at a cultural level, they were also at a military level. **Their mastery in the use of the recurve bow and cavalry led to a territorial expansion that drove the Assyrians to become a great military power and the creation of an empire** from 1350 B.C. until 612 B.C., which dominated the extension of the territory currently occupied by Syria, Lebanon, Turkey, Iraq and Iran.

If we think of horse archers, it is likely that the first thing that comes to mind is the image of those Mongolian warriors who conquered the Asian steppe until they reached Europe. **But the truth is that the Assyrians were the first to develop a bow with a recurve profile. The key date is 1800 B.C., when the first bows made of leather, ivory and wood, shorter than normal, originated. These recurve profile bows were more powerful than those of their Egyptian neighbors and, above all, more functional for use on horseback.**

The Assyrians were proud of these highly effective innovations. This is reflected in great works of art of the time, from the lioness wounded by arrows, found in the Palace of Nineveh, to the stone carvings of Assyrian archers now on display in the British Museum. Over time, however, the military might of the Assyrians had little to do with the innovations of the Persian Empire and the feared arrows of the archers of Xerxes I.

2.- Although at the time the notion of literature as such did not exist, these texts collected epics and other mythological narratives of the Assyrian civilization on clay tablets.

2.5 Persian civilization

«Honor to those who in their lives guard and defend Thermopylae. Never straying from duty; just and upright in their actions, not exempt from mercy and compassion; generous when they are rich, and even if they are poor, modestly generous, each according to his means; always telling the truth, but without holding a grudge against those who lie. And even more honor is due to those who foresee (and many foresee) that Ephialtes will appear and the Persians will finally pass».

Thermopylae, Constantino Kavafis.

In 2006, *300*, an American action film directed by Zach Snyder, hit theater screens. The film adaptation of Frank Miller's comics tells the story of how King Leonidas and his 300 Spartan warriors fought to the death against the Persian god-king Xerxes I and his army of more than 100 000 soldiers. The cry of «This is Sparta!» is surely one of the most famous quotes in 21st century cinema.

Although the film was criticized for its historical inaccuracies, there is one detail that, as we know from ancient texts, Snyder reproduced perfectly. When Xerxes' men reached the pass of Thermopylae in 480 B.C. C., besieged the Greeks with thousands of arrows. In the words of the historian and geographer Herodotus of Halicarnassus: «His arrows covered the sun and turned day into night, so he had to fight in the shade». Although it may seem an exaggeration, the truth is that, in 1939, the Greek archaeologist Spyridon Marinatos discovered a large number of Persian-style bronze arrowheads on the Kolonos hill in Thermopylae, a discovery that would confirm such an assertion.

ARCHERY

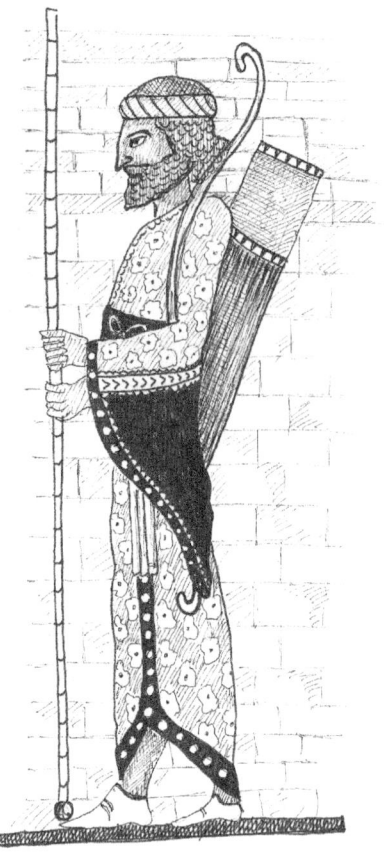

Persian archer

Spartans were not prepared for this attack for two reasons. The first was that they considered the bow and arrow an unworthy weapon, since it avoided hand-to-hand combat; the second is that they were not aware that the Persians had managed to develop a more powerful bow than those previously known, and whose use required less effort.

As we have seen, the evolution of the bow and arrow has been, in large part, the result of improvements to existing bows, the result of contact with other people. So it was with the Persians. The Persian Empire reached its height between 539 and 330 B.C., reaching the south of Europe. As they gained territory, the Persians also defeated the Assyrians, who they would weaken as a result of successive wars. **If the Assyrian bow was an improvement on the Egyptian one, the Persian was a refinement of the Assyrian into a much more effective weapon. It was a traditional, symmetrical and recurved bow, made with ibex, gazelle or deer horn. The rope was made from fallow deer or ox tendons, mixed with some natural adhesive. Once the bow was assembled, it was covered with bark, either fine leather or sharkskin, and finally parchment to protect it from moisture.**

In addition to the Persian territorial expansion, which led to contact with numerous cultures and people, there were also people originating from Central Asia and Southern Europe who migrated to the area of present-day Iran. Nomadic, Scythians, Sacians and Sarmatians people, all considered excellent archers, who contributed innovations that improved both the bow used by the Persian army and the techniques of warfare, including the addition of excellent archers to the ranks of cavalry.

The Persian bow and the use of horse archers brought great victories to the Persians, beyond the battle of Thermopylae. For example, during the reign of the Parthian dynasty (from 247 B.C. to 224 A.D.) the battle of Carrhae took place, and a confrontation against the Roman Republic fought near the city of the same name (now Harran, Turkey) in 53 B.C. The heavy Roman infantry could not compete against the skill and agility of the horse archers defending their territory from the invasion of Marcus Licinius Crassus, proconsul of Syria.

From the year 550 B.C. until the Islamic Revolution of 1979, the Persian Empire was ruled by ten different dynasties. What did not change over the centuries was the use of the Persian bow; although it was improved over the years, its fundamental characteristics were maintained until 1820, when it began to be replaced by firearms. And it can be affirmed that the use and development of the bow made by the Persians was the most important of all people we have explored so far and, therefore, of the history of the bow and arrow that concerns us.

The Persians left us an important legacy. It was their idea to form a universal empire, a goal to which many people throughout history aspired. It was due to the Persians that the use of currency in commercial transactions also became widespread. Zoroastrianism, the religion practiced in the Persian Empire, intimately explored the concepts of good and evil, and how man had individual freedom to choose between the two. In addition, if there is something that the Persian people were characterized by, it was for showing total tolerance for the culture and customs of the people they conquered over the centuries.

However, there was a society that Persian military skills, as well as their bows and arrows, and their values of tolerance and inclusion could not defeat: the Scythians.

2.6 Scythian civilization

In 1978 Tim Cope, adventurer, writer, tour guide and speaker, was born in Australia. Since 2004 he has been exploring the former Soviet republics. Cope says that of all the objects he has hoarded throughout his travels, his favorite is a hundred-year-old Kazakh saddle decorated with silver and traditional motifs. The explorer affirms that this object «symbolizes the intimate relationship that exists between man and horse in the Eurasian steppe».

Scythian archer with his bow

In addition to being intimate, the relationship between man and horse in the steppe is historical. From the 9th century B.C. until the 4th century of our era, the area of Central Asia and the territory that today make up Ukraine and Russia were inhabited by the Scythians, a group of people of Iranian origin, Nomadic shepherds and breeders of riding horses. Their first appearance in history dates back to the 7th century B.C., when the Scythians allied themselves with the Assyrians to fight against the Medes.

The Scythians never developed a method of writing, which is why what little is known about their origins, customs and civilization comes from ancient texts, from Latin and Greek sources to the Bible. The texts of the historian and geographer Herodotus and the physician Hippocrates narrate how the Scythians were descendants of the god Zeus himself: they say that Dallas, the first king of the Scythians, was the son of Hercules, son of Zeus and Echidna, a half-woman, half-serpent monster who lived alone in a cave and was the companion of the fearsome and deadly serpent Typhoon.

They are also mentioned in the book of Genesis (10, 2:3). The Hebrews believed that the Cimmerians, ancient equestrian nomads who, according to Herodotus, inhabited the area of the Black Sea and the Caucasus, were descendants of Gomer, grandson of Noah, and were also the mother tribe of the Scythians. The book also mentions that Japheth, son of Noah, was the father of Magog, a Scythian breeder of horses and camels that served as pack animals in Asia since ancient times.

It is possible that the lack of development of a method of writing contributed to the fame of the savage people that the Scythians had created among their neighbors. This reputation was also based on his brutality when it came to warfare. The «bowmen», as the Scythians were known, used to leave no survivors in battle, and their bravery and agility prevented even the Persians from conquering them.

In the year 514 B.C., Darius I, King of the Persians, commanded 700 000 men to cross the Danube until they reached the Ukrainian steppes. The Scythians, great warriors, had a very particular way of waging war. Strategic withdrawals, poisoned waters, burned pastures...

After several weeks, the Persian king sent a message to the Scythian king:

> Strange king, for what reason do you run away? You can face my army openly if you consider yourself powerful enough and if not, you must bring me offerings of land and water and submit to me.

To which the king replied:

> I have never run away from anyone, I just keep traveling just like we do in times of peace. If we do not face you it is because we do not have farms, crops or cities to defend. But if you want to fight so much, search the graves of our ancestors and then you will have your answer. Until then, everything will remain the same.

Neither the number of Persian warriors nor the threats managed to scare or intimidate the Scythians, who ended up responding by besieging the Persians with a hail of arrows, stating that they were excellent archers and horsemen, perhaps the best in the region and the epoch. From a very early age they were trained in everything related to horses and the bow and arrow. They ate on horseback, they fought on horseback and they died on horseback. It did not matter that, over time, so much equestrian activity caused sterility and impotence in men. Such was the importance of the horse in the life of the Scythians, including in death, that when a Scythian died riding his steed, a hundred horses were sacrificed to make the journey to the other world with the dead.

The fame of the Scythians went beyond their ability to balance on stirrupless mounts. **From those horses they were able to shoot arrows with a mastery that made archery great. The Scythian bow was a double-curved one that was relatively short compared to those that later people would develop.** It had a recurved shape and was very powerful, as well as comfortable to use on the animal's back. To transport weapons in combat, the Scythian horsemen carried a special container that the Greeks called *gorythos*, where they also carried a straight-bladed dagger or sword made of bronze or iron, which accompanied a leather shield reinforced with metal plates. Generations and generations of combat on horseback made the Scythians great strategists and military technicians.

Thus, towards the 7th century B.C., the Scythian town reached its maximum splendor. They invaded Syria, Palestine, and even reached the land of the pharaohs, who avoided the invasion thanks to the payment of tributes. Territorial expansion brought them into contact with Greece and the Assyrians, two people who exerted a powerful influence on Scythian art, through which the Scythians were able to reflect the importance they placed on both the horse and war. They represented numerous scenes of hunting and combat between animals, such as felines or bears attacking their prey, which reflected the warrior character of the Scythians, as well as their taste for realism and naturalism.

However, over the centuries the Scythians lost power. Alexander the Great, who had conquered the same Greek civilization that had so influenced Scythian art, defeated them in 329 B.C. in the battle of Jaxartes, which took place in the area now occupied by Uzbekistan, Tajikistan, Kyrgyzstan and Kazakhstan. With this, the empire of Alexander the Great removed the immediate threat that the Scythians had posed for other people. The Scythians, in turn, began to decline until they disappeared.

2.7 Greek civilization

At the hour Ulysses stripped off his rags, jumped to the great threshold with the bow and the quiver full of swift arrows and, spilling them before their feet, he spoke in this way to the suitors: «Now this tiring contest is finished; now I will aim at another target where no man has ever shot, and I will see if I hit it for granting me such glory the god Apollo».

The odyssey, Book XXII, Slaughter of the suitors.
Homer.

Ulysses (or Odysseus), King of Ithaca, had been away from his land for twenty years: the ten that the Trojan War[3] lasted, and another

---

3.- According to Greek mythology, the Trojan war pitted a coalition of Achaean armies against the city of Troy and its allies. According to Homer, author of great epic poems such as The iliad and The odyssey, the conflict in Troy was triggered by the abduction (or escape) of Helen of Sparta by the prince Paris of Troy.

as many that took him to return to his kingdom[4]. Disguised as a beggar, Odysseus went to his faithful servant Eumaeus, who explained to him the situation of the kingdom: everyone thought he was dead and his beloved wife, Penelope, after two decades of waiting, had been forced to look for a substitute king among the nobles who wanted her.

Yet Penelope had never given up hope that her husband would return alive, and she kept putting off the moment of their wedding. For this reason, in order to make the choice of her future husband impossible, she organized a very particular archery contest: the suitors, coming from Ithaca and other nearby cities, had to shoot an arrow through the eye of twelve axes lined up, using for it the bow of the missing king. Whoever won would get his hand.

Ulysses was a unique archer, and her wife knew that none of those present would be able to overcome the challenge, without suspecting that her husband would arrive just in time for the contest. Athena, goddess of war, combat strategy and skill, helps Ulysses to draw up a plan and take revenge on his wife's suitors, and he entrusts himself to Apollo, god of the Arts and protector of sailors, shepherds and archers. After entering the contest and winning it, Ulysses reveals himself and assassinates all the suitors with an arrow, thus recovering the love of his wife.

The odyssey is not the only Greek play in which the bow and arrow play an important role. Homer's *The iliad*, dated 762 B.C., narrates the last 51 days of the Trojan War and focuses on Aquiles' wrath, who is a great archer and a war hero. In the Book XXIII of the epic poem, the funeral games are held in honor of Patroclus, Achilles' best friend, who died at the hands of the Trojan king. Among chariot races, boxing, wrestling, combat, shot put and javelin, there was archery. These games are reminiscent of the first Olympic Games, held in 776 B.C.

Although the mythology of ancient Greece was full of references to the bow and arrows or the feats performed thanks to them, and even though goddesses such as Artemis (Diana in ancient Rome), goddess of the hunt, were always represented carrying bows and arrows, in

---

4.- Homer recounts in The odyssey that Ulysses' return journey was hindered by the fury of Poseidon, god of the sea, in revenge for his son Polyphemus, whom Ulysses leaves blind for trying to escape being devoured by the cyclops.

Greece archery was more famous as a sport than as a technique of warfare. Even the first Olympics had a certain mythological reference.

Artemis goddess

The games of 776 B.C. were celebrated in honor of Heracles (Hercules), a Greek demi-god famous for his skills with the bow. For example, the work of the Italian painter Luca Cambiaso (1527-1585) shows one of the twelve labors of Hercules[5], the arrow-killing of the Stymphalian birds, voracious creatures that ate human flesh, had claws, wings and metal beak and used their feathers as arrows. Hercules' mastery with the bow was also reflected in Greek art. In fact, visitors to the Louvre Museum (Paris, France) can enjoy kraters that represent the demi-god with his bow.

What is striking about these works is the size of the bow, small compared to Heracles. Although over time the bow was incorporated into the Greek army as an indispensable force, for a long time it was considered only as an auxiliary force for the hoplite infantry[6], famous at the time. In fact, despite the importance of the bow in mythology, and the fact that it was the hallmark of many of the Hellenic deities, ancient Greece never had a great tradition of archery in battle.

Contrary to what happened in the Middle East, the armies of Greece, the cradle of western civilization, were characterized by their preference for hand-to-hand combat, and their combat weapons were developed based on this priority. The toxotas, the archers of ancient Greece, used short bows, the same as those represented on the kraters of the Louvre. They also carried a small sword with them, ideal for close combat. As elements of personal defense they used a small light shield called a pelta, which over time evolved into a light armor with a small round bronze shield and a brace for the left elbow. However, unlike other warriors, the Toxotas did not wear a helmet.

The Greek ranks compensated for the lack of archers with the use of other weapons, such as javelins or light cavalry. However, as the

---

5.- Hercules was married to princess Megara, the daughter of the King of Thebes. Together they had three children. But one day Hercules, victim of an attack of madness, ended their lives. Repentant for the atrocity, he went to Delphi to consult the oracle of the god Apollo what he should do to atone for his crime. The answer was that he had to go to Tiryns and put himself under the command of King Eurystheus. When Hercules arrived and explained the reason for his visit, Eurystheus began to worry about the throne. Therefore, he decided to get rid of Hercules by entrusting him with twelve tasks, each one more complicated than the previous one. Actually, the twelve labors of Hercules represent twelve stages that man must overcome on the way to liberation, knowledge and truth.

6.- The hoplite was a citizen-soldier of the Greek polis. His name comes from the term hoplon, translated as «armor item» or «equipment». He was a heavy infantryman, as opposed to the gymnet and psylos, who were light infantrymen.

Greeks interacted with other people, either through trade or wars (as happened with the Persians), their generals became convinced of the importance of the use of the bow in the military field, since that in frontal engagements bows and arrows were much more flexible and adaptable than the rigid phalanx formations of the hoplites. Thus, the bow and arrow began to be used on a large scale during the Peloponnesian war (431 to 404 B.C.)[7].

It was the Cretans, members of the Peloponnesian League and allies of Sparta, who focused on the development of the bow and arrow. Although the fighting was still hand-to-hand, the Cretans carried a compound bow and a small bronze shield. Their light combat clothing facilitated the movement of the soldiers.

This review of the history of archery in ancient Greece cannot be closed without mentioning Alexander of Macedon, known as Alexander the Great. Thanks to the military mastery of his father, King Philip, and their own strategic skills, the Macedonians were able to conquer Greece and expand their empire through Egypt and Persia, all the way to India. Of course, it also helped that the Macedonian army had a section of archers and cavalry in its ranks, as well as a powerful phalanx.

Such was the power of the empire of Alexander the Great that they say that Julius Caesar himself envied him, and to ratify it, the moment in which the politician and military man cried in Hispania before the statue of Alexander, lamenting that he had not been able to achieve as many feats as he did at the same age, has gone down in History.

7.- The Peloponnesian war was a military conflict between the cities formed by the Delian League (led by Athens) and the Peloponnesian League (led by Sparta).

2.8 Roman civilization

«One-third or one-fourth of the youngest and most capable soldiers must also exercise at the post with bows and arrows built expressly for this purpose. Instructors of this weapon must be carefully chosen and diligently applied to teach men to hold the bow in the proper position, draw it hard, keep the left hand steady, draw accurately with the right, direct your attention and your gaze to the target and take aim with equal precision both on foot and on horseback. But this is not acquired without great dedication, nor is it preserved without daily exercise and practice».

Compilation about military institutions.
Flavio Vegecio Renato.

Thanks to *Epitoma institutorum rei militaris*, a treatise written by Flavio Vegetius Renato on the military uses of the Roman army, we know that the ancient Romans were trained in the use of the bow and arrow. These works are important, since the Roman civilization had much in common with the Greek, including the little relevance that their armies gave to the bow and arrow.

The Romans revolutionized the concept of war and its strategy by changing the impenetrable Greek phalanxes formed by lancers to the legions, smaller units that gave the army greater speed, independence and mobility. Far from being equipped with bows and arrows, the legionnaire's military equipment consisted of a short sword and small spears; the use of arrows was restricted to protecting cities, and it was the Scythians, famous for their archery skills and for being excellent horsemen, who were in charge of this task. However, as the Roman legions advanced in their territorial conquest, they became convinced of the effectiveness of the bow in the military field.

Roman archer on horseback

Although the bow and arrow were not very well established in Europe, the Romans encountered the people of the Middle East around the 63 B.C., when they had to intervene in the area of Judea (now Palestine) to put down a war of succession and ended up occupying the territory that makes up Syria today. The Romans encountered enemies who were great archers and horsemen. So much so that in 53 B.C. the troops of the Roman Republic were defeated by the Parthian Empire in the battle of Carras.

Given the fact that spears and swords did not match for the fast and functional compound bows used by the Parthians, the Romans soon realized that conquering territory would require a new approach. For this reason, the Roman legions began to incorporate the bow into their ranks and use it in war. So rapid was their incorporation that bows have even been unearthed in Roman tombs found in Wales, a territory where the Romans arrived in 43 A.D., barely ninety years after the battle of Carras. It is also believed that the Romans gave these bows to the local inhabitants, who were still unaware of their existence.

Although the Roman bow never became the weapon of choice for Roman soldiers, and did not have a good reputation, armies did incorporate archers into their ranks. The bow developed by the Romans was recurved and compound, and the arrows had metal tips, made from bronze or iron. In battle, archers used to stand behind the infantry, shooting their arrows over their companions.

Despite these adaptations, nothing could prevent the progressive decline of the Roman Empire. To the attacks of the tribes of the Middle East, militarily superior in terms of the use of the horse and the bow, were added the ambushes of the barbarian people on the northern border of the empire. Roman arrows could do little against the Britons, the Celts or the battle-hardened Germans. These people did not use bows, because they considered an act of cowardice not to face their opponents hand to hand; they valued the bravery of the warrior to such an extent that the only protection they used for battles was an oval shield and a sword, as they did not fear combat wounds. Celtic finds confirm that the bow was used solely for hunting. In their bows they engraved a symbol that represented life and death, which was believed to protect hunters and give them luck when killing animals and providing food to the villages.

Neither could the Romans prevail over the Huns, a nomadic and semi-nomadic people from Central Asia. Although the Huns initially helped the Romans against the Germanic people, becoming allies, they eventually created a power structure and empire so vast that, by the 5th century A.D., came to threaten the two capitals of the broken Roman Empire, Rome and Constantinople, despite the fact that the Romans even offered money to prevent the Hun advances, which they rejected.

2.9 Hunnic Empire

«There are blows in life, so strong... I don‹t know! Blows as from the hatred of God; as if before them, the hangover from everything suffered was pooling in the soul... I don‹t know! They are few; but they are... They open dark trenches in the fiercest face and in the strongest loin. Perhaps they will be Attila‹s barbarian foals; or the black heralds that Death sends us».

The black heralds.
César Vallejo.

Back in the 5th century A.D., the Roman Empire dominated Europe and part of Asia, without imagining the changes that were coming and that would predict the fall of their empire.

The people from Eastern Europe, such as the Alans, the Ostrogoths and the Visigoths, began to make inroads into Roman territory, displaced by a nomadic people of great archers and horsemen who devastated everything in their path: the Huns. Such was the efficiency and power of these armies from Asia, that they came to put in check the greatest empire the world had known up to that time.

You can't talk about the Huns without mentioning the mythical Attila, also known as «the scourge of God». From 434 A.D. until his death in 453 A.D., Attila ruled the largest empire of his time: from the Caspian Sea and part of Russia, Central Europe to the Black Sea, and from the Danube River to the Baltic Sea. Among his great military feats, he counted invading the Balkans twice and becoming one of the staunchest enemies of the Roman Empire after besieging Constantinople (present-day Istanbul, and at that time the capital of the eastern Roman Empire). He was about to become Roman emperor, and only the defeat at the battle of the Catalaunian Fields (451 A.D.) prevented him, marching with his troops until reaching ancient Gaul (France), from where Emperor Valentinian III would expel him in 452 A.D.

Who were the Huns? The truth is that the origins of this town respond more to speculation than to proven facts. The most accepted theory is that this nomadic people appeared around the 4th century in the area that today corresponds to China and Mongolia, but precisely this nomadic way of life has made it difficult to find archaeological remains that could reveal something more about how they expanded, where they settled and how they lived before Attila.

It seems that the beginnings of what later became the Hun Empire were simply migratory movements.

Ancient China spent years unsuccessfully trying to subdue the Huns, who, tired of so much harassment, moved west in search of new territories where they could continue their way of life. This took them not only to Europe, but to the frigid lands of the Altai, in the mountains of Siberia, where in 1986 archaeological remains of this people were found.

How did a nomadic people from Eastern Asia become a military superpower that could stand up to the Romans, both in the east and the west, at the end of the 5th century? The Altai finds offer a clue: the Hun bow. **Our journey through the history of archery has shown us how the Huns were not the first to develop the compound bow. However, the Hun bow was original, as it included improvements and adaptations of the bows used by the people of the Middle East with whom the Huns were in contact.**

The main improvement of the Hun bow was that bone had been added, both in the handle, to prevent bending, and at the ends of the blades, thus acting as a lever. Compared to the bow used by other nomadic people, the Hun bow was considerably larger in size; while normal bows measured about 80 centimeters on average, the Hun bow reached a size of between 130 to 160 centimeters.

These very particular characteristics of the Hun bow made it notably superior to the one used by the people who inhabited Europe at the time, such as the Germans, the Bretons or the Gauls. They were the first to realize the effectiveness of the bow of the Asian conquerors, who saw their warriors fall dead even before they could draw their bows.

However, despite the superiority of the Hun bow and its greater power and range thanks to its size, it was also a more difficult bow to handle on horseback, and it could even hinder horsemen who needed to draw their sword in combat.

That is why the Huns tried to compensate for this lack of functionality by creating asymmetrical bows, with the lower part shorter than the upper part. Although this asymmetry made it a more inaccurate bow than its opponents, this did not prevent the Huns from conquering all territory in their path.

In addition to being well equipped with bows and swords, Hun soldiers were excellent horsemen. From early childhood, the Huns learned not only to make their elaborate bows, but also the art of horsemanship. The combination of both activities was essential to survive as hunters in the Asian steppe, first, and in their war tactics, later.

Thanks to their handling of weapons on horseback, a perfect combination, they were able to attack their enemies quickly and by surprise. Before then, rains of arrows caused countless casualties from a distance, thus paving the way for the moment when the Hun horsemen broke through the enemy ranks with their swords. With these techniques, the Huns managed to surprise the Indo-European people they encountered in their path and the Roman legions that had been invincible until then.

Much has been written about this people and their almighty leader, Attila. We will never know how much legend there is in the greatness that they contributed to giving the bow and arrow, but what we do know for sure is that, although other people, such as the Sarmatians and the Parthians, also stood out for their use of these weapons on the backs of a horse, none of them managed to put the powerful Romans like the Huns in check and at their feet.

ARCHERY

Hun horseman in combat

CHAPTER III

THE MIDDLE AGES

«The governor calls us outlaws,
but I say we are free».

Robin Hood

Is there a more endearing character that generates more sympathy than the beloved Robin Hood? Without having verified his historicity, he has become one of the most famous archers, and his figure has been the subject of controversy throughout the centuries. It is likely that he did not exist as such, but surely at some point there was a man who inspired and gave rise to the legend. It is not known for sure if that person was of noble origin (Robin of Locksley or Longstride), or simply a soldier who returned to England after having fought in the crusades, but the truth is that, ever since the 14th century, the English ministrels sing the exploits of this character, who stole from the rich to give to the poor.

A century later, European songs carried by word of mouth the legend of William Tell, who would end up becoming a symbol of Swiss independence. Tell lived in Bürglen, a municipality in the canton of Uri, Switzerland. On one occasion, the famous archer turned against the governor, Hermann Gessler, when he was walking with his son and refused to bow before a hat hanging from a pole in the town square, symbolizing authority of the Holy Germanic Empire. Knowing the fame of his crossbow marksmanship, the governor conditioned his freedom on Tell being able to shoot an apple placed on the head of his own youngest son. Tell, of course, was right. However, when he was asked why he was carrying two arrows, the answer was clear: had he missed, he would have shot the second arrow into the governor's heart. For this insolence, Gessler ordered his imprisonment, but taking advantage of a storm, the archer managed to escape, reach the governor's castle and kill him.

The exploits of Robin Hood and William Tell serve to show how in the Middle Ages, a historical period that goes from the fall of the western Roman Empire (476 A.D.) to the discovery of America (1492) or until the fall of the Byzantine Empire (1453), archery was no longer just a battle weapon. The bow and arrow enjoyed a good reputation, and archery was beginning to become popular as a sport in all social strata, especially in the area of what is now the United Kingdom.

The Middle Ages will be the last glorious age of archery, since over time the bow and arrows would begin to fall into oblivion due to the arrival of firearms. Although the first references to gunpowder date back to the 12th century, and an English manuscript dated 1326 already spoke of firearms, it was not until the 16th century that this type of weapon, easier to use and more lethal, replaced the shot with a bow as a weapon of war and hunting. However, those early weapons had less range, speed, and penetrating power than the bow, even though marksmen were easier to train than archers. For this reason, the change was not immediate, and the professional archers began to disappear only when the muskets developed greater shooting power.

In the next chapter, we will explore the role the bow and arrow played in the Middle Ages, before firearms were introduced. More specifically, we will focus on Europe, including England, where the best bows of the time were made; and Al-Andalus, Spain, then dominated by the Arabs.

3.1 Europe in the Middle Ages

«Giving him the city is not my decision or that of any of its inhabitants; we have decided of our own free will to fight, and not to save our lives».

Constantine XI, last emperor of Byzantium.

On May 29, 1453, Constantinople, the capital of the eastern Roman Empire and the last of its vestiges, fell into the hands of the Turks, led by Mehmed II, son of sultan Murad II. The decline of the Byzantine Empire had begun with its decision to remain neutral while European troops fought against Saladin, sultan of Egypt and Syria, during the Third Crusade, which would lead the crusaders to storm the city in 1204. Although at first Mehmed II had agreed to respect the borders of the Byzantine Empire, in 1451 the Byzantine emperor dared to ask the sultan for an annual payment for the support of an Ottoman prince he was holding as a hostage. Furious, Mehmed II began preparations for the siege of Constantinople.

The fall of the Byzantine Empire is, along with the discovery of America, one of the events that marks the end of the Middle Ages, which had begun ten centuries earlier, with the fall of the western Roman Empire. On September 4, 476, a German mercenary named Odoacer expelled a young Romulus Augustus, who would be the last emperor of an empire already in decline due to corrupt governments, unable to deal with barbarian incursions on its northern borders.

The Middle Ages brought many changes. The first of them, and perhaps the main one, was the implementation of a new social system based on a bond of servitude and on the payment of tributes by the people to the nobility and the church in exchange for protection: vassalage. During this time the church amassed unprecedented political and religious power, especially in Rome. For their part, the feudal lords (high and low nobility) transformed society almost in its entirety, exercising absolute control over the land, which they used not only as a source of material and economic resources, but also as hunting grounds, leisure, and even as currency.

During this long period the wars followed each other. On the one hand, the feudal lords got into fights to occupy territories and castles, in order to get more resources to protect themselves and prosper. On the other hand, the church focused all its efforts on fighting the enemies of christianity: the Muslims. In addition to the reconquest of Al-Andalus (Spain), Rome dedicated many of its resources to the crusades, a movement created by European nobles united under the banner of christianity to conquer Jerusalem, the holy land for Christians, and that at the time it was under Muslim control.

Many of these battles were won thanks to the skill of medieval archers, making the bow and arrow a key element of European armies. Although during the late Middle Ages archers continued to use the simple bow, later they would incorporate a recurve and compound bow, very similar to the one used in the Middle East, and that we have described in previous sections. However, the performance of these bows was quite poor and the main cause was the lack of skill of the medieval archers, who instead of opening the bow and bringing it to the face, shot from chest height.

After the siege of Jerusalem in July 1099, Christians managed to take the city. The conquest did not last long; and, in fact, the First Crusade was the only successful one. In 1187 the sultan of Egypt, Saladin, took Jerusalem with his army. And, although two years later, the famous Richard Lionheart launched the Third Crusade, little could be done. Muslim recurve bows were far superior to European bows, including the English longbow.

3.1.1 The bow in medieval wars

«Twenty horsemen joined the ranks of the invader; the men, and also the horses, were clad in iron; one of the horsemen shouted:
—Is Earl Tostig here?

—I do not deny being here —said the Count.
—If you are truly Tostig —the rider said—, I come to tell you that your brother offers you his forgiveness and a third of the kingdom.
—If I accept —Tostig said—, what will the king give Harald Hardrada?
—He has not forgotten him —answered the rider—, he will give him six feet of English soil, and since he is so tall, one more.
—Then —said Tostig—, tell your king that we will fight to the death.
The horsemen left.
Harald Hardrada asked thoughtfully:
—Who was that gentleman who spoke so well?
The count replied:
—Harold, King of England».

Heimskringla.
Snorri Sturluson.

On October 14, 1066, in the vicinity of Hastings, a coastal town in the English county of East Sussex, a Norman minstrel named Taillefer sang the first verses of what we now know as *The song of Roland*, the oldest European epic poem written in the romance language and the most important French medieval epic composition. With the chords of *The song of Roland*, the battle of Hastings began, from which William the Bastard, duke of Normandy, would emerge as William the Conqueror, King of England.

The song narrates how at the end of the 8th century the Emperor Charlemagne, King of the Franks, crossed the Pyrenees to besiege the Spanish city of Zaragoza, then Muslim. Back in France, the two responsible for covering the rear of Charlemagne's troops are ambushed in Roncesvalles and die. Charlemagne's reaction to the death of young Roland stands out. Such is his pain that it was even speculated that Roland was the illegitimate son of the emperor, since only a man can mourn so bitterly the death of another if it is his son.

The minstrel did not know that after that battle that began on October 14, 1066 another death would also be mourned, that of King Harold II (Harold), son of Jodwin, the Saxon King of England, who lost his life on the battlefield. An arrow entered his eye and pierced his skull, knocking him off his horse. His death freed the English throne, which was occupied by duke William of Normandy. In other words, it was an arrow that decided the fate of England.

Normans and English crossed paths that day about 11 kilometers from what is now the English city of Battle. The Anglo-Saxon troops of Harold II were on top of a hill, in a formation of «shield wall», practically impassable for enemies. So much so that the Saxons believed their victory in battle was assured: the Norman arrows and the charges of their infantry and cavalry had been repulsed by the Saxons. But with the euphoria came an overconfidence, the Saxon troops abandoning their tight formations to pursue the fleeing enemy factions.

Astute duke William of Normandy realized that the undisciplined Saxons were easy prey. He commanded his cavalry to attack those who scattered, and his archers to fire on what remained of his rival's formations. The Saxons were finding it increasingly difficult to keep their defense cohesive, and it was becoming easier for the Norman archers and crossbowmen to soften the ranks of their enemies and open gaps that the cavalry could exploit to wreak as much havoc as possible.

When King Harold was struck by an arrow and died, only the most stalwart of him were left to defend his corpse. Most of his men fled, pursued by the Norman cavalry. The body of the late monarch was given to his wife Edith, daughter of the duke of Mercia, to be buried in sacred ground. William of Normandy, chivalrous, did not accept the money offered by the mother of Harold II for the body of her son.

On Christmas day of 1066, William was crowned King of England in Westminster Abbey. The chronicles of the time tell that the coronation occurred amidst great revolts, which were suffocated with great bloodshed and burned villages, something that for many was a prediction of the new king's entry into hell.

While the weeping of Charlemagne came to us through *The epic song*, the events of the battle of Hastings and the Norman conquest of England are literally woven into history. The Bayeux Tapestry, also known as the Queen Matilde Tapestry, the most important textile work in the medieval world, narrates how William of Normandy, William the Bastard, went down in history as William the Conqueror. But, in addition, the tapestry gives us a fairly approximate idea of what the battles of the time were: numerous archers and their arrows can be seen in the work.

However, what the loom does not show is that archers were not very numerous among the troops of the European armies of the time. The reason? That although the bow and arrow were much cheaper than armor and a sword, it was very expensive to train professional archers. As a result, most archery units were made up of men recruited from the peasantry, who could be paid much lower wages.

However, the bow had a period of splendor during the Middle Ages, more specifically after the so-called Hundred Years War. If the English had learned anything after centuries of war, it was the effectiveness of the bow as a weapon of battle, especially when combined with other weapons. But at the start of the Hundred Years War[8], King Edward III realized that it was going to be very difficult for him to pay the high salaries of professional archers. Therefore, he was inclined to reduce his services to a minimum and opted to hire mercenaries. It was from the battles of Crécy and Poitiers that the tables turned, and archers became highly sought after.

On a beautiful morning in August 1346, some 7000 men led by Henry III of England waited for French troops on a hilltop between the French towns of Crécy and Wadicourt. The goal was to take Paris. For this, the English king had two groups on foot and horsemen. Among them were archers arranged in an arrow and behind, near a forest, chariots and horses with additional supplies of arrows.

The French troops arrived around noon, and it didn't take long for the battle to start. The English perfectly combined the charges of their cavalry with their archers, experts in handling longbows. Defeating the Swiss crossbowmen who were fighting for the King of France was an easy task, especially considering that during the confrontation it began to rain, and the strings of the Swiss crossbows lost their elasticity when wet. In addition, the English knights dismounted their mounts and, despite their armor, fought on foot alongside the archers.

8.- The Hundred Years War was an armed conflict between the kingdoms of France and England that lasted from May 24, 1337 to October 19, 1453. The reason for the conflict was to resolve who would control the additional lands that the English monarchs had accumulated from 1154 in French territories, following the accession to the throne of England of Henry II Plantagenet, count of Anjou.

The victory against the French was flagrant and produced many casualties in the French nobility (about 4000 dead, 1500 of them knights). The English victory did not mean the end of the war. Between 1346 and 1353, the Black Death ravaged Europe, shaking the economic and social foundations of the Old World. After this pause, the war resumed in 1354, and the English again defeated the French troops, this time in Poitiers.

Edward of Woodstock, prince of Wales, swept across southern France, from Bordeaux to Languedoc, and on September 19, 1356, defeated the French army at Maupertuis, at the south of Poitiers[9]. As Carl Grimberg relates in his *Universal history*, it was during this battle that the young prince, barely 16 years old, was decorated as a knight by his father, Henry III of England, and became known as The Black Knight, because of the color of his armor. During this battle, the French king, John II of France, was captured and taken to London, thus beginning a period of great instability in France.

As had happened at Crécy, this time the French also suffered a humiliating defeat. **The English longbow allowed each of the 3000 archers to shoot between 10 and 12 arrows per minute, which created a veritable rain of arrows (of tens of thousands per minute) and fell on the horses of their opponents, much less protected than the knights.** The injuries to the horses caused a disbandment among the French troops, creating confusion and chaos among the warriors. However, despite the fact that the prince of Wales was able to deliver the *coup de grâce* by capturing King John II, on this occasion, the French troops did manage to block the path of the English and forced them to fight to avenge previous defeats.

How was this possible, seeing the lethality of English arrows? The question is even more pertinent if one takes into account that the French troops were greater in number than the English. The answer is simple: the significance of the archers was merely tactical.

In the battle of Poitiers, the English had, in addition to the archers who had positioned themselves in some bushes that were very difficult for the French cavalry to access, about 4000 knights, 4000 horsemen and 1000 infantrymen. The French, for their part, entered the battle

---

9.- It is also known as the second battle of Poitiers, the first being the battle in which Carlos Martel defeated the Islamic army.

mainly on foot. Only two groups, each of between 200 and 250 men, under the command of marshals Jean de Clermont and Arnoul d'Audrehem, made up the armored cavalry. However, some of Clermont's men reached the hedgerows where the English archers and some foot soldiers were. The other group managed to envelop the English on the left side.

According to an English chronicle of the time, «French cavalry were well protected by steel plates and leather armor, so that arrows either broke or ricocheted skyward, falling on friend and foe alike». The English archers had broken through the lines and were able to fire towards the less protected sides. This is how historian Jonathan Sumption describes it, considered the best specialist on this subject:

> «The longbow, the key to most English victories in the fourteenth century, played a relatively minor role at Poitiers. The archers were quite efficient against the initial French cavalry attack and during the final phase, when the French were driven down the hill from Audley and the Captal de Buch, but they were much less efficient against men on foot than against the enemy horses».

Eight years later, the battle of Auray took place, possibly considered the bloodiest among the wars of the Breton succession[10], and derived from the Hundred Years War. Again, Sumption gives us a description of the role played by the bow and arrow:

> «Despite their great numbers, the English archers contributed almost nothing to the success of the battle. Arrows were never as effective against men on foot as they were against horsemen, whose horses wore no armor and were easily frightened. The French also gradually improved their way of fighting on foot and learned to protect themselves better. Du Guesclin advanced his well-armored men in dense ranks under a roof of shields[11]. Froissart relates that

---

10.- During the war of the Breton succession (1341-1364) the succession of the Duchy of Brittany was decided, disputed by the Monfort and Blois families.
11.- Bertrand du Guesclin, known in Spanish as Beltrán Duguesclín, was a French soldier and constable. Du Guesclin is famous in France for his role in the Hundred Years War against England, and also in Spain for having intervened in the campaigns that Henry II of Trastámara, the Fratricide, held against his brother, King Pedro I of Castile.

the archers threw down their bows, with which they had achieved nothing, and charged into combat».[12]

In a well-commanded unit, the effectiveness of the archers meant that the enemy had to give up the most important attacks, those carried out by the heavy cavalry. The knights, who wore increasingly heavier armor, lost mobility and lethality. Therefore, knights have been known to die in combat not from war wounds, but from heat stroke caused by the high temperatures of their armor.

This lack of mobility caused by the armor was actually an advantage for the archers, who were less well armed and protected than the knights. They attacked with swords, long knives and hammers, while arrows did not have the same effect as a rifle at close range. Although there are accounts of vicious executions of archers when fighting hand-to-hand with knights, these are probably just exaggerations, as archers had the same fighting will and stamina as light foot soldiers.

In fact, although the English bow was not a miracle weapon, it was capable of penetrating the coats of mail of the 14th century. However, the effectiveness of the arrows also depended on the protection of the adversary. An illustration of the battle of Mühldorf (1322)[13] clearly shows the different armor worn by the different ranks of the armies of the time, as well as the conical helmets that left the face unprotected. Even so, it is perceived how the dukes and counts were much better protected than the escort squires, who had to settle for older and heavier armor.

The European nobility did not understand that wars had reached such complexity that the use of various weapons was required. It took time for the French to learn it, but, by the battle of Formigny (1450)[14], they had already obtained two small cannons, which dislodged the English archers and opened the way for the French cavalry. Although they faced some 3000 archers and 800 foot soldiers, French casualties were between 200 and 300 men.

12.- Jean Froissart is one of the most important chroniclers of medieval France. His chronicles have been considered the most important expression of the chivalric revival that took place in France and England during the 14th century. He is one of the main sources for the first half of the Hundred Years War.
13.- The battle of Mühldorf or Ampfing was fought on September 28, 1322, near Mühldorf, between Austria and the Duchy of Bavaria.
14.- The battle of Formigny took place at Formigny, near Carentan, France. It ended up in a decisive French victory over the English on April 15, 1450.

A scene from the Hundred Years War

On May 8, 1360, in the French village of Brétigny, France and England signed peace through the Treaty of Brétigny, also known as the Treaty of Calais, and began a nine-year truce within the Hundred Years War. As a result of this agreement, England gained control over Calais, where the base of operations was established until the 16th century, and France had to give up Aquitaine, among other territories, in exchange for the English king, Edward III, renouncing the French crown.

This truce led many archers to be employed as mercenaries in other European conflicts, in order to survive. The so-called «free companies», groups of mercenaries that acted independently of any king or lord, mainly went to Italy, where the richest cities, Florence and Genoa, were in constant conflict.

The Italian chronicler Filippo Villani praises the English above all for their heavy armor, brought from France and relatively new to Italy. In order to dazzle their enemies, the servants of the Italian generals were ordered to polish these armors, which earned the armies the nickname of the White Company.

Villani, on the other hand, spoke of the famous archers thus: «It was found that their best assaults were made at night and by stealing, and that they held out in battle. But his success was due more to the cowardice of our people than to their own bravery». This did not prevent mercenary companies, such as Astrorre Manfredi's Star Company, from soon defeating formal armies.

An objective analysis of the battle of Poitiers must mention that the victory of the English also has a lot to do with the arrogance of the French nobility, who rushed at their enemies without any kind of tactics or discipline in their ranks. But they were not the only ones. The battles of Nájera (1367)[15] and Aljubarrota (1385) exemplify how the Castilians were not much more modest. Similarly, that very audacity was the cause of the bloody defeat in the battle of Nicopolis against the Turks.[16]

The battle of Nájera is another example of the superiority of the English archers and their fearsome longbows against any kind of force, since it was the first in which they had to face the light cavalry, against which they were just as deadly and efficient as ever. Unfortunately, the French strategists would not learn this bloody lesson until almost a century later, and the insistence on frontally attacking the archers would cost France thousands more dead.

15.- The battle of Nájera, also called the battle of Navarrete, was fought on Saturday, April 3rd, 1367. It was an episode of the first Castilian Civil War, which pitted King Pedro I of Castile against his half-brother, Enrique de Trastámara, who aspired to the throne, involving Castile in the Hundred Years War.

16.- The battle of Nicopolis, also called the Nicopolis Crusade, took place on September 25, 1396, and pitted the forces of the Ottoman Empire against a coalition of Hungarians, Vlachs and French, with the latter losing.

On August 14, 1385, in a hot evening, the battle of Aljubarrota took place near the town of Aljubarrota, in central Portugal. The hosts of Juan I of Castile, supported by the French cavalry, clashed with the army of Juan I of Portugal, who had 500 English archers, mercenaries belonging to the Order of the Black Prince, considered as the best archers of the time, among their soldiers. Although the Portuguese army was smaller in number, they positioned themselves on a hill, allowing the mercenaries to attack the French cavalry with their arrows and wreak such havoc that a general rout ensued. The Castilian soldiers also fled, and were annihilated by the pursuers and the townspeople.

Once again, and just as it had happened in Clércy and Poitiers, the English bow prevailed over the cavalry troops. The morning after the battle, the magnitude of the massacre was confirmed: the victory was so overwhelming that Portugal obtained independence from it. To commemorate the triumph, Juan de Portugal ordered the construction of the Monastery of Santa María de la Victoria in the Cadiz town of Puerto de Santa María.

Thirty years later something similar would happen at the battle of Agincourt, which took place in Artois, in northern France. **On October 25, 1415, the English and French troops clashed again, this time due to the wishes of Henry V of England to recover his rights as monarch over the territories that the English crown had in France. The troops commanded by the English monarch, made up of almost 10 000 men, consisted almost exclusively of well-trained archers.** They carried with them longbows made of yew, elm and ash, with a draw weight of between 80 and 150 pounds and an effective range of 180 meters. At 50 meters, these arrows could already pierce armor, so the 4100 mounted archers, each armed with 48 arrows of which they could fire between 10 and 12 per minute, created a veritable and lethal cloud of projectiles that did not let the enemy breathe. These arrows opened the way for the 3700 infantrymen. As a historical curiosity, it should be noted that most of the English soldiers fought only with a loincloth from the waist down due to dysentery that they had contracted in a previous siege.

The French army was led by marshal Juan de Marigne and constable Carlos d'Albert. It was far more numerous than the English, numbering

17 800 men, including a corps of 2000 archers and crossbowmen[17]. It seemed, however, that the French troops had learned nothing from the mistakes of their compatriots in past battles, and they threw themselves into the fight without any kind of strategy or discipline. Of course, the result was disastrous: 7000 French and 500 English remained on the battlefield. Once again, the longbow had determined the fate of the English troops.

The one who also wanted to count on the services of the English archers for his battles was Carlos the Bold, almighty duke of Burgundy. The result, however, was not what was expected. In both the battles of Gransonsen (1476) and Morat (1477) his troops were no match for the Swiss infantry, who were much more agile on foot than the heavily armored knights. Likewise, at the battle of Stokeen (1487), the last in the Wars of the Roses[18], 2000 lansquenets[19] and Swiss achieved a similar victory over the English, despite their superiority in terms of men, weapons and the strength of their archers. Even so, the English remained convinced of their superiority on the battlefield, claiming that one English archer was worth the same as 20 French archers.

In 1544 King Henry VIII of England tried to emulate past victories and invaded France. He not only realized that his legendary archers could not do anything, but he found that he had to recruit and hire thousands of lansquenetes, Spanish arquebusiers and mercenaries from many other countries. As a result of this failure, his daughter, Elizabeth I (Elizabeth Tudor), decreed the exclusion of the bows in the recruitment of the English army.

Despite this, the debate about the advantages and disadvantages of the bow in battle continued in England until the end of the 16th century. In fact, in 1590 a proponent of the arquebus noted that while bullets frightened men more, arrows frightened horses even more. And it is that the English longbow, the famous longbow, was a really unique bow.

17.- Other sources consulted mention 10 000 men from the English side and 30 000 French.
18.- The Wars of the Roses was a civil war in England that intermittently pitted members and supporters of the House of Lancaster against those of the House of York between 1455 and 1487.
19.- Name given to some German mercenaries who operated between the 15th and 17th centuries.

3.1.2 England and the longbow

As we have already verified, if there are people in the west that have displayed archery and raised it to national glory, it is the English. Robin Hood would not have been able to carry out his deeds, prowess and heroics without his English bow (longbow), made out of English yew (or Spanish, or Austrian); the English troops would not have been able to achieve this success, victories that were often unthinkable in situations that defied military logic, if commoners had not become deadly and insidious shots that responded cheaply, efficiently and from a distance to the superiority of the enemy knights, trained over decades in combat.

The English longbow was between 1,5 and 1,8 meters, sometimes reaching the 2 meters. This allowed English archers to cover enemy troops with barrages of arm-length arrows, in waves spaced only a few seconds apart, and at a distance and speed unknown until then.

The longbow, known as the machine gun of the Middle Ages, caused terrible damage among enemy ranks and managed to undermine the morale and fighting spirit of the enemies.

What few know, however, is that the English longbow is actually of Welsh origin. Seeing its effectiveness and the number of English lives the weapon claimed during the invasion of Wales at the end of the 13th century (1280), the devotees of Saint George incorporated a large number of Welsh archers into their troops. In addition, they began to train their recruits (including peasants) in the technique of archery.

Nevertheless, making bows and arrows was not an easy task. In fact, it required rigorous planning and, above all, a lot of time, since the process of building a bow could take up to four years. Tree branches had to be cut in the coldest winter months and then cured for a minimum of one or two years. During those months the sap of the tree was found only in the trunk, which prevented the branches from cracking when they dried. The tree preferred by the English for the construction of the longbow was the yew. So much so that when overexploitation caused the yew to become scarce in British territory, they began to import Hispanic, Austrian and Bavarian specimens.

The Spanish yew from the valleys of the Pyrenees and the Sicilian yews were especially appreciated as a raw material since, growing in drier climates, they were slower growing and had tighter veins. Castilla tried on several occasions to prohibit the sale of yew to the English, but ingenuity allowed them to get away with it. They began to import Spanish wine, but the condition was that it had to be shipped in yew barrels, which of course they later disassembled and whose staves they used to build their bows. Castilla tried by all means to prevent fraud and began to make shorter barrels; the English, for their part, learned to make their dreaded bows by joining two barrel staves together.

War needs brought with them an abusive felling of European yew trees. As the valued trees disappeared in Central and Northern Europe, the price of yew battens continued to rise. From the year 1483 the price of a hundred strips of yew rose from 2 pounds sterling to 8; in 1510, the same hundred pieces cost £16, something few could afford. For this reason, bows began to be made in elm, ash, walnut, poplar or willow wood, which, although less elastic and resistant, were cheaper.

To preserve the flexibility and elasticity of their bows, they were kept disassembled until before the start of the battle. Stringing and unstringing bows was a quick task, and archers used their thighs to bend the bow slightly and place the strings, usually made of hemp, linen or silk. However, sources of the time say that the great efforts to tighten the ropes ended up creating characteristic muscle hypertrophies and bone deformities in the upper limbs. To protect the strings from snow and rain, they were kept inside archers' hats or helmets, as the oil from the scalp kept them naturally oily, and ready to tighten.

Arrows were made from the same materials as bows. These were about 80 cm long and weighed between 60 and 100 grams. It was customary to harness them with goose or goose feathers.

For the glue that joined the feathers to the shafts, fish bones, pieces of skin and cooked bones were used, which were boiled until obtaining a paste to which quicklime was added to thicken. Of the tails of animal origin, the most appreciated, effective and sought after, especially among the troops of the Ottoman Empire and other people of the Middle East, was the Muscovy (or Isinglass) tail. It was obtained from the throat mucous and swim bladder of the sturgeon[20]. However, whenever possible, and especially when large quantities of arrows were made at one time, it was preferred to use birch resin, which was stronger and more effective than animal-derived glues, especially when it came to moisture. As a vegetable glue, the English also used a sticky secretion obtained from the precious blue flower of the common bluebell, our wood hyacinth.

Despite being a laborious task, the English quickly realized that the bow was a relatively cheap piece of craftsmanship to make and maintain. In addition, it allowed the armies to train hundreds of peasants in the art of archery, in fact, the feudal lords instituted one day a week to train the peasants in the use of archery: Sunday, the only day in which their work and tasks were interrupted. The practices were carried out on land near the church, esplanades where archery contests and competitions were also held in which stumps of old trees were used as targets.

This training was necessary because the use of the bow in battle could be even more decisive than the spear, which also required more complex instruction for its optimal use. The ideal time to shoot the arrow was when the enemy was about 300 meters away. The archers shot from a herse, a barrier of wooden stakes covered with sharp nails that protected shooters from the cavalry charges. At that range, the arrows fell in a sharp parabola that had a devastating effect. So much so that the rain of arrows was called the rain of death.

20.- At present, the sought-after fish adhesive is mainly used in the restoration of medieval illuminated codices. Its price is around 1500 euros per kilo if it comes from the best species of sturgeon, which are those from the Caspian Sea.

ARCHERY

English archer with his longbow at the Battle of Crécy

To shoot faster, archers placed their arrows in front of them. The rate of fire reached eight shots per minute, even reaching twelve or fifteen per minute in case a rapid and massive rain of arrows was needed. The usual, however, was six shots per minute, something that was already exhausting and painful for the fingers, since the bows weighed between 90 and 180 pounds (41 - 70 kg). This meant that the average rate of arrows per minute tended to decrease as the battle progressed, especially considering that trading speed of fire for accuracy was sometimes a priority.

According to the sources of the time, an archer required at least eight years of training to be able to live professionally from his bow. Among those who made their living with the bow were the English and Welsh mercenaries, who were happy to offer their services in exchange for a soldier. To their salaries it was necessary to add what they obtained from the spoils of war, from looting enemies annihilated by their arrows, or their share of the ransoms paid by nobles and rich captured as prisoners during battles. Therefore, it is not unreasonable to say that professional archers earned a good living, better than those who were part of the lower echelon of medieval society.

In medieval Europe archers were not the only ones employed as mercenaries. Stingers, halberdiers and spearmen also offered their services to the highest bidder. However, none of these weapons could rival the bow. Only the arrival of the crossbow temporarily endangered the existence of the bow due to its greater precision and range, but its slow reloading and less versatility prevented it from being replaced.

Such was the importance that the British monarchs gave to the longbow that the tower of London came to store large batches of thousands of complete weapons and wooden slats for their realization, as an arsenal for the Crown in times of war. For example, in 1342, Edward III had accumulated in the tower 7000 bows and three million arrows, ready to invade France; in 1360, the arsenal of the tower had 15 365 bows (4062 decorated bows and 11 303 unpainted); and 567 404 arrows ready to be used (4000 wooden strips to make bows and 23 646 bundles of arrows). Even in the middle of the Renaissance, when portable firearms were booming, King Henry VIII stocked up on some 40 000 yew wood slats for bow making, which he bought from the duke of Venice in 1510; in 1534, the armory of the tower had 30 000 bows stored.

The longbow continued to be the main weapon of both the English ship crew and the militia troops (a third of them still used bows and arrows, compared to two thirds who used firearms), and of the garrisons of the coastal castles, called to resist any Spanish landing on British soil.

The success of the longbow and arrow was such that the English came to identify themselves with their favorite weapon of war. At the end of the 18th century, still in full imperialist ecstasy of the Victorian era, the practice of archery became one of the greatest distractions of the British wealthy class. Either out of nostalgia for past military glories, or because of the reminiscence of the heroic deeds of the English army reflected in the works of sir Walter Scott, an unusual fervor for archery was awakened. It is even known that some of the archery clubs and societies that emerged during this time in the country organized meetings and dinners in which the members of the club came dressed as in the Middle Ages, in a nostalgic attempt to recreate the medieval time and clothing.

The most important of these societies is surely the Royal Toxophilite[21] Society, founded in 1790 and whose patron was the prince of Wales, the future George IV. Many of the rules governing archery competitions in the UK today were dictated by this society. But, above all, these clubs served to foster social relationships among their members. Being part of these exclusive clubs was a wonderful opportunity to introduce themselves in society, a space in which the promising landed and mercantile bourgeoisie could display their wealth, and where it was common to give free rein to flirtation. Although the English were characterized by hindering women's access to most of their social clubs, this was not the case in shooting clubs, since it was usual for women to attend the numerous competitions and archery contests. Photographs of the time show corseted women wearing huge hats, something that, despite not being very comfortable for shooting arrows with precision, was a symbol of social status and has been transferred to our days, where we can see them wearing the most various headgear at Ascot races. Archery also occupied an important place in the education and leisure of the offspring of wealthy families who, paradoxically, entertained themselves with an activity that had once been the work of commoners.

However, the supremacy of the English longbow ended in 1595, when the English Crown ordered all bows stored in arsenals to be replaced by firearms. In fact, the last written record that remains on the use of the arrow and the bow in combat dates back to 1644, and it refers to the use of the longbow by royalist troops during the English Civil War, at the battle of Tipper Muir (today Tibbermore), in Scotland.

Legend has it, although there are reasons to believe that it is true, that the duke of Wellington himself wanted to create a body of longbow shooters with which to overwhelm Napoleonic troops who, despite threatening Europe, did not have protective armor or breastplate for battle. To his surprise, he was unable to find enough well-trained archers in all of England with which to recall ancient medieval glories and once again do battle with the French.

21.- Bow-lovers, in classical greek.

3.1.3 The Normans

The historical enemy of England, along with Spain, has been France. The French people have their origin in the Franks, a people of Germanic origin who little by little conquered the territory that we know today as France. Tired of the Viking invasions and the destruction that this entailed, they agreed with the invaders to cease the attacks in exchange for the donation of the territory of Normandy. The Normans take their name from this territory.

Although we have seen that the longbow was a Welsh creation, it was the Normans who originally introduced the bow to England through the troops of William the Conqueror, duke of Normandy. As we have explored in previous sections, the duke invaded the island and, at the battle of Hastings, (October 14, 1066) defeated the Saxon troops of Harold II using military strategy and ordering his soldiers to shoot skyward as their only way to penetrate the wall of the Saxon shields, Viking type.

The Saxons made little use of archers, but were able to copy the longbows with which the French had attacked during the battle of Hastings. That is to say, the adoption of the longbow among the English was the result of realizing that their weapons had become obsolete in the face of Norman innovations.

As we have seen, the longbow awarded great victories for the English and for those armies that decided to count on their services for battles. Among them, we have included the battle of Nájera, which took place in Spain, a Spain that at that time was in the process of reconquering the territories that had been taken by Muslim troops.

3.2 Spain, islam and the Arab bow

«Bows do much more damage to the enemy than any instrument of war, more than once a single arrow defeated an army; knights fear a single archer, champions tremble before him. With a single arrow fired at your enemy you can get rid of him from a distance. It is known from experience that one archer can more than a hundred men. For this reason, those who understand wars consider that each arrow is a man; if a man has a hundred arrows he is counted as a hundred men. The enemy fears the archer more than the sword or the spear because he deals much more damage».

Abd Allah, Andalusian sage.

In the year 711 A.D. the troops of the Umayyad Caliphate, commanded by the Berber Táriq ibn Ziyad, arrived in the Iberian Peninsula. The Muslims defeated the army of the Visigoth King Rodrigo (also known as don Rodrigo) in the battle of Guadalete, who had come to power a year earlier after a violent civil war. His rule of the peninsula lasted almost 800 years, until in 1492 Muhammad XII (known as Boabdil el Chico), King of the Nasrid kingdom, the last of the Taifa kingdoms, handed over the city of Granada to the catholic monarchs, Elizabeth and Ferdinand.

After conquering Spain in just fifteen years, the Muslims would come to enter present-day France, and their idea was to continue conquering territory in Europe. However, the Muslim advance on the continent stopped on October 10, 732 when Carlos Martel, the grandfather of the well-known Charlemagne, defeated the troops of the valí (governor) of Al-Andalus, Abdar-Rahmanibn Abd Allah Al-Ga-Fiqi, in the first battle of Poitiers, and the Muslims withdrew to the peninsula and the Balearic Islands.

The Muslim invasion changed the history of Hispania. In addition to the architectural, scientific and literary advances that the Arabs introduced in the Peninsula, the curved bow also stands out, very similar to that of the Asian steppes, much more advanced than the antiquated monolithic bows of the Visigoths, and very easy to carry on horseback. The Turks, who came from the steppes of Central Asia and were great archers, converted to Islam and were the main people in charge of expanding the Muslim empire and its military power throughout the Mediterranean. And it is that, in addition to being great archers, the Turks were accomplished horsemen. From the age of 6 or 7, children were trained in archery on the back of a sheep, in order to achieve aim even on the move. The Muslim cavalry was among the most notable of the Middle Ages. The Arabs had invented stirrups, which gave riders enough support to turn and shoot in different directions, which gave them an advantage against the enemy armies, who succumbed to the rains of Islamic arrows.

The Muslim arrows produced such terror in their enemies that in the Byzantine churches of the 9th and 10th centuries, the masses ended praying to God to save people from them. **However, by the 12th century, the Arab bow, short and recurved, but fast and powerful, and ideal for horseback riding, had been widely incorporated into light cavalry.** Such was the terror produced by Muslim arrows in their enemies, that in the manuscript *The book of wonders and Arcana on attack response, victory, and secrets as it pertains to outpost archers*[22], collects the following story, a story that, despite not leaving the honor of archers in a good place, serves to describe the importance of the bow in their battles:

> A man who was a great skilled and famous archer and one of the best handlers of the foot bow (crossbow), was shooting arrows from behind the wall in a certain fight in which the inhabitants of Al-Andalus participated. He was participating in the fight by shooting a rain of arrows that caused great mortality among the enemies, when he and other archers were encouraged by someone to come out of the tower and thus be able to shoot their arrows closer, on the strongest of the enemies and their reinforcements. An unfortunate circumstance caused the place where he was to be destroyed and he had to move to another where he met a black man who was more than ten cubits tall and brandished in his hand a lance resplendent as flashes of fire. The black uttered such a cry that he startled the archer and startled him so that he dropped what he had in his hand. He regretted the fact, but God granted him what he asked for and delayed his death. He responded to the black's stratagem with another that consisted of showing the, man the bow, making him see that he had saved his life thanks to the fact that he had thrown it to the ground. The poor black man

---

22.- This work, by an unknown author and of Andalusian origin, is believed to have been written in Almería. There are two incunabula of this book, one in Berlin and the other in Rabat, both written in clear and careful oriental handwriting.

actually believed that the archer had not wanted to kill him and kissed his hand as a sign of respect and gratitude. Then the black man withdrew, thinking that he had saved his life, but the archer shot an arrow at him when he had turned his back, so that blood began to flow from his chest and he fell to the ground. The archer returned to his stand biting his fingers with guilt as he thanked God for saving him.

Archery had great fame and symbolism in the Islamic world. In fact, several surahs (verses) of the Qur'an refer to the high regard Muslims held for the bow and arrow. So it is with this one, in which Jibril (the archangel Gabriel) explains to Adam the symbolism of the bow and arrow:

«Gabriel said to Adam: this bow is the power of God. This rope the Majesty of Him. These arrows are the wrath and punishment of God inflicted on his enemies...»[23].

The prophet Mohammed, who is said to have been a great marksman and possessed six bows, said: «You do not shoot when you shoot, it is God who shoots».

The bow became one of the Muslims' preferred weapons when carrying out jihad, thinking that they were touched by the hand of God. Some caliphs even imposed on their subjects the learning of archery, both for adults and children. In the 14th century, Al-Andalus, Ceuta and the Moroccan protectorate had 44 yasalt (archery ranges), and some cities had up to nine of them, some reserved for high-ranking public officials and monarchs. Its popularity was such that it came to be present at burials: when an archer or warrior died they buried him with his bow and a handful of arrows in his hand.

The Arab bow evolved throughout history, and was given different forms and names depending on its place of origin.

According to Al-Qayyin Al-Yawziyya, a Sunni Muslim jurist and exegete of the Koran, handheld short bows are classified according to their provenance. Three groups are distinguished:

23.- Quote provided by M. A. González.

- Arab bows (*hiyaziyyas* or *wasitiyya*).
- Persian bows, used by the Islamic troops of Syria and Egypt.
- Turkish bows, somewhat thicker than Persian bows.

These short bows were mainly used by light cavalrymen. However, among infantrymen, in battles in cities or fortifications, and in naval warfare, the intermediate bow, *al-watiyya*, was used. This bow was halfway between the Arab shortbow and the Frankish longbow or the English longbow. The measurements varied depending on the type of battle in which it was to be used and the materials used for its construction, which could include yew, ash, cork oak and wild olive wood, although the most used were orange wood, apple and quince.

Parts of the bow

We have commented how the name given to the bow depended on its place of origin, the way it was made and the materials used in its manufacture. However, regardless of all of the above, the Arab bows had the same components:

- *Furda* or *Furdad*: it is the notch or crimp where the string is tied at the end of the bow.
- *Dufr* o braid: the area of the bow that goes from the furda to the tip of the bow.
- Shaft: distance between the bow handle and the *furda*.
- *Watar*: is the name given to the rope. The strings were made of different materials depending on the type of bow, the fabrication place or the time of the year. The most common materials were silk (used in winter and kept in Chinese oil to prevent it from drying out), thread, leather or animal nerves, especially old camel sinew (*feshat*). Both leather and nerves were especially recommended for summer. The fundamental difference between European and Arab bows was precisely the strings. Muslim women were generally made of 50 or 60 threads of silk, a material that is as light as it is resistant. Once the arrows

were made, rows of tendons were used to intertwine them at the ends of the blades, thus preventing the deterioration of the silk. Silk, widely used in the Muslim world, came from China, a country with which Muslims had had trade relations since ancient times.

Arab arrows

Arab arrows were short, with a spindle-shaped shaft and somewhat wider in the middle, which gave them better aerodynamics. To facilitate its launch, Muslim archers used an implement made of bone or horn that allowed them to support the arrow somewhat further back regarding to the body of the bow. To shoot, Muslim archers used to hold the bowstring with the thumb, protected by a thimble made of horn or bone.

The parts of the Muslim arrows were the following:

- *Qidh*: the shaft or body of the arrow, made of wood or cane. The types of wood varied, but the wood of the apricot tree was especially valued for its hardness, while the cane from Syria (Qasab sami) was valued for its good quality. The most widespread theory among Arab archers was that the lighter the arrow, the greater its range. However, the size of the shaft varied depending on the type of bow that was going to be used and the archer's preferences, although the standard measurement was one cubit and with a width equal to that of a finger (without specifying which one).
  The Arabs also decorated or marked their arrows on the shaft with their name or with feathers to identify them after the battle and make a count of their merits.
- *Nasil:* is the tip of the arrow. This point was built with various materials: copper, lead, bone, animal horns, stone or hardened wood. The most popular material, however, was iron. The points varied depending on their size, their use, etc., but they were always well-sharpened. In addition, they had retractable fins that, when removed, caused large hemorrhages in the body of the victims.

- *Rud*: the notch or crimp from the shaft to the tip.
- Laughter: the feathers of an arrow. The feathers were of natural origin and were adhered with natural glues extracted from animals and plants. Once glued, these were adjusted with silk threads around the feathers. The most recommended feathers, due to their higher quality, were those of the eagle, vulture or raven. However, it was recommended that feathers from different birds should never be mixed on the same arrow, so for mass production, feathers from other more common birds were used.

As a historical curiosity, and because it is a practice that the Amazonian tribes still use today for hunting, the Arabs used to use poisoned arrows in combat. Saqalibas (slave archers) poisoned arrows with fruits called mabiellos, while Sudanese archers poisoned arrowheads with the blood of yellow snakes. These poisoned arrows were used above all by the high Arab leaders. Of course, not all archers carried the same number of arrows, it was the high officials who had the most, twenty-five, which they carried in their quiver The *al-ahza* was the name given to the last arrow in the quiver, and it was the one in the worst condition.

About the quivers

The quivers were found in different shapes and were made of different materials, in most cases of thick fabric, leather and/or wood, and almost always finished with careful decorations, adorned with very valuable stones and metals.

The quivers were part of the archers' uniform, and received different names depending on the origin of the archer, its manufacturing material and its use. Among those names were: *yafir*, *yafar*, *dafra*, *zugar* and *zugariyya*. It is believed that the quivers known as thugar have their origin in an area of the same name in Syria, where red and gold cartridge belts were also made. This name became popular during the time of Caliph Al-Hakam II (Córdoba 915-976), when the narratives of the time mention that archers used *zugariyyas*.

The care of the bow

Fortunately, several accounts of how Arab bows were made and cared for have survived to this day, especially in the texts of the Granada-born writer Ibn Huday, who wrote on military subjects by order of the caliph. Ibn Huday made recommendations on how to use and preserve the bow depending on the time of year.

In winter, he used to say, drawing the bow is dangerous both for the archer and the bow, which, due to the cold, is more taut and runs the risk of breaking. Therefore, before shooting, it was important to put the bow in the sun so that it softened and smoothed out. If the day was very cold, the solution was not to shoot, unless the archers were involved in a military campaign. In summer, the bow should be kept in cool places, protected from the sun, and used only when it was not hot. For this reason, the Arab archers created a special case to store their bows.

During the battle, the Muslims were on horseback. To prevent the bows from deteriorating, they were kept on the lower side of the horse. There they remained protected from meteorological phenomena and were always at hand.

The bow and medical advances

One of the great things about Al-Andalus is that he allowed the coexistence of Christians, Jews and Muslims. In cities like Toledo, for example, the Cristo de la Luz mosque combines Muslim with Romanesque art. If it is also taken into account that the mosque is not far from the Jewish quarter, the coexistence of three cultures is clearly appreciated, each with its customs and traditions, and this exchange gave rise to great advances in science and literature.

On the contrary, it was not so in the field of medicine, an area of knowledge in which the religious tradition had a clear influence. While among the Christian population medical advances were practically non-existent, the Jews focused on the pharmacopoeia, the compilation of recipes for products with real or supposed medicinal properties. The Arabs, for their part, prohibited quackery and «magical» practices that occurred in Christian territories and dedicated themselves to developing general medicine, and especially surgery.

The medical advances that occurred in Al-Andalus, even more so in the time of the Umayyad Caliphate, are mainly due to three causes. The first is combat casualties. As in any war, there were wounded. This implied that either the wounded had to be transferred to the main cities, or they had to be treated on the battlefield. Therefore, two types of hospitals were developed. On the one hand, there were mobile hospitals, so it is known that there was a specialized medical corps that always accompanied the Muslim troops.

In this sense, it is worth highlighting the fundamental role played by women. During the prophet's lifetime, those wounded in combat were cared for not only by companions, but also by women who accompanied armies. As the knowledge of medicine was perfected, women began to carry out more specialized tasks, such as drawing arrows from easy wounds, healing wounds from cuts caused by swords, repositioning bones, and even collecting and burying the dead. It can be said, therefore, that Muslim women were the forerunners of today's nurses. The Muslim chronicles of the time offer much data about these activities, as well as Qur'anic evidence that approved these activities.

Soldiers who could not be cared for on the battlefield were taken to the big cities (*coras*) on mules or camels. There, great doctors from the retinue of the caliphs worked together, who considered it a duty to put their knowledge and skills at the service of warriors and society in general.

In addition to being forerunners to a great extent of the military administration, the Muslims were aware of the importance of protecting themselves against epidemics. These were cruel to the armies and in turn were transmitted by them to other populations. In the short term, this implied the loss of men and means; in the long term, it could have social consequences if the epidemics spread among the civilian population. For this reason, and in order to cut epidemics and common diseases derived from misery, Muslims made an effort to preserve the purity of their food and drinks, and placed great emphasis on the need to preserve hygiene and personal cleanliness, something that did not happen in Christian territories. Such were the hygiene conditions that it was even a norm among the Muslims of Al-Andalus to wash the dead, in addition to praying for them if the situation allowed it.

The prophet Mohammed had made it very clear in his teachings: «cleanliness is part of faith». This philosophy of hygiene and purity had concrete effects. For example, the city of Córdoba had more than 700 public baths, which the Andalusians of the time had access to, much cleaner in body and clothing than their Christian contemporaries.

Nevertheless, this did not prevent large epidemics from devastating Al-Andalus and Northern Africa. Between the years 804 and 805 an undetermined epidemic killed a third of the population by famine; a little less than a hundred years later (900-901) the plague made an appearance, which worsened between the years 915 and 916, when the famine was joined by another epidemic and the epizootic (more commonly known as the avian flu); five years later, a new epidemic of plague occurred that lasted a year, and it repeated at the end of the century (983-984) during the time of Almanzor.

The Andalusian texts that have survived to the present day speak of these and many other advances of the time. For the topic that concerns us in this book, military medicine texts are particularly interesting. The development of surgery and medicine were of great help to Muslim military advances, and although many of the texts compiled below may not be a perfect translation or may even be taken out of context and somewhat incoherent, they show conversations that perhaps they are very similar to those that today's doctors maintain when they treat their patients and tell their colleagues about their exploits.

In battle, there were mainly sword, spear, projectile and fire wounds, and of course arrow wounds. Knowledge about arrow wounds, the type of injuries they produced, and the type of procedure they required was widely documented. But, to carry out their work in a good way, doctors also had to know the different types of existing arrows. According to the Cordovan doctor Al-Zahrawi in his writings:

> Arrow wounds vary both by the type of arrow and by the part of the body where it penetrates. As far as the differences between its different types are concerned, there are big and small ones; some have concave points and others hard points: some have three points and others four; some have tabs and others have corners.

The difference due to the part pierced by the arrow is double for any of the main or hollow organs such as the brain, heart, liver, lungs, kidney, intestine, bladder, and others of this kind. When one of these arrows pierces an organ of this kind and you observe the signs of death that I will describe to you later, you must avoid the extraction of the arrow, because the death of the wounded person generally follows, but when you do not see these deadly signs and the arrow has not penetrated deep into the organ, then you need to remove it and treat the wound[24].

Sometimes the arrows were poisoned, in which case they were very serious, the doctor had to observe changes in the color of the wounded body that could appear black or livid.

As we said, Arab doctors had the obligation to spread their knowledge. That is why Al-Zahrawi gave details (not suitable for the squeamish) about the various surgeries he performed, as well as treatments used to heal wounds. These texts are believed to have been addressed to medical students:

> One man was injured by an arrow in the inner cingulate corner of his eye near the base of his nose and it was removed through the other side, below his earlobe, and he recovered with no damage to his eye.
> I also extracted from a Jew another arrow which had penetrated near and below the lower eyelid. The arrow was hidden from view with only the small *al-qidh* (shaft) end sticking out, but it was a large arrow from a compound bow, with a smooth square iron point. The Jew recovered, his eye did not suffer any damage. I also took another arrow from the throat of a Christian, it was an Arab arrow, one of those with two points. I separated the jugulars, since it had penetrated deep into his throat, and gently maneuvered it until it was extracted and the Christian was saved and recovered.
> I also took another arrow from a man who had been shot in the abdomen and we thought he might die from this. But when I stayed with him for about thirty days and his condition did not change, I

24.- Taken from www.arcomedievo.es

wrapped the meat around the arrow and maneuvered it out and he recovered and nothing bad happened to him. I also saw a man who had been wounded in the back by an arrow, it had closed over him. After seven years the arrow came out through the birth of his thigh. I took an arrow from an officer in the service of the authority, who had hit him in the middle of the nose, slightly crooked to the right. The arrow had completely disappeared. He called me to heal him three days after he had wounded him with the arrow. I found the arrow wound very narrowed. I explored it with a fine probe and did not feel it. But the patient felt a tingling and pain below his right ear. I expected that tickle to be caused by the arrowhead. I applied foments of attractive and maturational force on the spot with the intention that it would become inflamed and a sign of the arrow would appear, so I could cut where it was. But nothing occurred at the site to indicate that the arrow had landed there. I continued to apply the foments for many days and nothing happened. In the meantime, the wound was closed and for some time the patient had no hope of extraction, until one day he felt the arrow inside his nose and informed me of it.

Then I put caustic medicine on the wound for many days, until it split open. I explored it and felt the thin end of the arrow, which is attached to the shaft. Then I widened the wound with that caustic medicine until the end of the arrow came into view. It took me a long time, about four months. Then when the wound had widened, I was able to insert the tweezers into it. I tugged at it and moved it, but he didn't respond and didn't come out. I continued to manipulate gently and cunningly with all sorts of instruments, until one day I managed to grab it with solid tweezers and pull it out. Then I tended to the wound. The doctors were of the opinion that the cartilage in his nose would not recover, but I restored it. The wound was closed and the patient healed perfectly, he did not suffer from it at all.

As can be seen at the beginning of this excerpt, and in relation to the coexistence between the three religions that we spoke about earlier, Muslim doctors did not only cure Muslim warriors, but also Jews and Christians. And it is that, as part of their faith, Muslims should prioritize the human and religious character before conflicts.

The doctor Al-Zahrawi also spoke of more complex surgical operations, in which the arrow wounds were not very serious:

> The arrow must be removed by pushing it. When it enters the soldier's body, the arrow can be removed if it appears and there is no gravity according to army surgeons. Arrows are removed from body parts when they have been pierced, in two ways: either from the entry site or from the opposite side. From an arrow that comes out, the track of its trajectory is followed; the arrow must be visible, resting on a fleshy part in which case it must be extracted by pushing it. If it did not respond to traction it would break immediately; it should be left for a few days until the tissues have suppurated around it, then the extraction will be easier.

It is also known that army surgeons had both procedures by which to treat wounded soldiers and equipment, including tweezers and probes, to remove arrows if the wound was clean, although sometimes fingers had to be used. In addition, they had material to sew the wounds, bandages to cover them and drugs to treat infections:

> If the arrow is hidden somewhere in the body and is hidden enough to explore with a probe, and if you can feel it, then pull it out with an appropriate instrument. But if you can't get it out anymore because of the deep narrowness of the wound and there's no bone, no nerve, no blood, then cut it, rip it around until the wound is wide enough for you to be able to grab it and extract- the. And if it has two tongues by which it is helped, leave them free of the meat adhered around the wound, in the way that you can leave it free of the bandages; try carefully to break the two tabs and twist them until the arrow is free.

However, if the arrow has penetrated any soft tissue in the body, such as the brain, heart, lungs, stomach, or liver, it is recommended that the arrow is not removed for several days:

> If the fixed wound is in the bone of the head and has reached the ventricles of the brain and the patient feels any of the symptoms that were cited, then desist from removing the arrow, leave it like this for several days until the case is seen clearly. When the arrow has reached the meninges, death will not wait. If the arrow is only fixed in the substance of the bone and has not penetrated the meninges, and if the patient continues for a few days without any of these symptoms, then try to pull it out and remove it. But if it is very firmly fixed and does not respond to traction, use gauze around the arrow as I told you, so you will bandage the place until it heals.

However, as we have already mentioned, the arrows could be poisoned, which was an additional difficulty. In case of poisoning, Muslim doctors recommended:

> If the arrow is poisoned you must, if you can, draw it out and cut around all the flesh into which the poison has entered; then care for the wound with whatever is appropriate.

Al-Zahrawiva goes a step further and explains the procedure by which a poisoned arrow must be removed:

> When you want to extract an arrow from any part, use a circular movement of your hand moving the tweezers in all directions until you remove it, and use them with extreme delicacy so as not to break the arrow and thus make it harden, to remove it. If you are unable to get it out right away, then leave it for a few days until the tissues around the wounds rot.

The doctor Ibn Sinä does not recommend closing the wound when it is infected. However, when the infection stops, doctor Ibn Abbas Al-Mayusi advises to sew the wound and «when necessary, put on the wound a remedy for wounds, good plasters». Regarding medicines for wounds, Muslim doctors left several recipes for poultices from plants and tree leaves, in addition to their uses and indications, collected in their works.

The bow was so popular with Muslims that the *The book of wonders and Arcana on attack response, victory, and secrets as it pertains to outpost archers* puts in the mouth of Al-Mu'tamid, King of the Taifa of Seville, the following affirmation:

> You should know that a blessed and victorious bow, qurašî by its origin and typical of rulers[25], you will only see in the hands of people of aristocratic origin, noble nature, proud spirit and lofty intentions, while you will never see a standing bow except in hands of the ignorant fool, of short sights and poor intentions.

For this reason, when the use of the Muslim bow began to decline in favor of the crossbows of the Franks, there was some rejection by the more purist Muslim military. And it is that, as Ibn Hudayl narrated:

> God, may He be exalted, accorded his preference to the bow, above any other weapon. The prophet once said: «Every believer should aspire to have a bow and arrows».

25.- The prophet Mohammed was born into the tribe of the Quraichites, also known as the Quraish or Quraysh, a tribe that controlled Mecca. The Quraysh tribe was, paradoxically, the one that fought the first Muslims the most, forcing them to emigrate from Mecca to Medina in 622 A.D., thus updating the saying that «nobody is a prophet in his land».

CHAPTER IV

THE BOW IN THE ASIAN CONTINENT

In the previous chapter we have been discovering how, little by little, firearms and gunpowder began to displace the bow and arrow. However, the key and definitive moment came with the defeat of the invincible armada: in 1588, 10 000 English soldiers equipped with firearms mercilessly defeated the troops of Felipe II, whose army was made up mostly of archers, to whom they had entrusted an almost impossible victory. Two thirds of the soldiers died in the battle, returning to Spain a decimated troop. «I did not send my men to fight against the elements», Felipe II assured in reference to the bad weather, storms and currents that surprised them on the coast of the United Kingdom. But other elements that the Spanish king did not count on were those new and deadly weapons against which his selfless archers could do nothing. Military strategists were convinced: archery had become obsolete as a weapon in battle and was, compared to new developments, a relatively ineffective method of warfare.

While this was happening in Europe, on the other side of the world the bow continued to have a privileged place. During the Renaissance, numerous testimonies from European travelers told stories about how the bow and arrow continued to be the most important weapon in

Asia, America, Central Africa and the Arctic region. Explorers were not only discovering new places, new species of flora and fauna, new customs. They also discovered that archery had many more uses than battle and war.

The Asian continent harbored a secret: the different traditions of archery shared a vision of the discipline unknown until that moment in the west. The bow and arrow were not only weapons of war, but were also understood as a martial art and a method with which to achieve personal and spiritual development. The skill of archers was not measured by the number of casualties they caused in combat, but by their use in religious ceremonies, rituals and contests. To add mystery to the use of the bow in Asia, each country had different traditions, customs and equipment.

In this chapter we are going to explore the use of the bow and arrow in the territory that goes from present-day Hungary to the most remote corners of Asia. Mongolia, China, Japan, Korea, Vietnam, Tibet, Bhutan and even the inhospitable Siberian steppe: they all serve to explore a new conception of archery.

4.1 The Magyar bow

«Ajándék lónak ne nézd a fogát».
Hungarian proverb.

Literally translated, this Hungarian proverb says *don't look a gift horse in the mouth*. Beyond the linguistic curiosity that supposes that two languages as different as Spanish and Hungarian have such a similar expression, this proverb helps us to understand the importance that horses had for the predecessors of the Hungarians. And with the horse, inexorably, also came the bow and arrow.

Hungarian archer

Like the Mongolians, the Hungarians were great horsemen and archers, and also feared enemies. The comparison may seem unnecessary, since Hungarians are often associated with Hungary, a country located in Europe. However, the genesis of these people is not European, but apparently they are originally from central Asia; more specifically, present-day Hungarians are believed to be descendants of the Magyar. The Magyar tribes were settled in the area of the Ural Mountains (Russia) until the end of the 9th century when they conquered the plain of the Carpathian Mountains (the so-called Pannonian plain, which originated after the drying of the Pannonian Sea during the Pliocene) and established the principality of Hungary. One of the existing theories is that the Hungarian demonym comes from the old Russian; more specifically, from the word *Yugra*, which was the name given to the area between the Péchora River (in Russia) and the Ural Mountains. Another theory is that the Hungarian demonym has its origin in the Ogur or Oguric languages (Bulgarian languages, also called

Lir-Turkic). This theory is based on the customs, diet and phonetics that they share with the Turks. More specifically, its origin is associated with the words on-ongur, which literally translated mean ten tribes or, even more interesting, ten arrows.

Like the feared Mongolians, the Magyars were also avid users of the bow and arrow, which they shot from their horses. Such was their mastery on horseback that to this day it is debated whether it was they or the Mongolians who devised stirrups (which were later perfected by the Arabs and imported to the peninsula). As we have seen before, the stirrups gave the archers total mobility on horseback and allowed them to shoot in all directions.

The Magyar bow continues to be built today, and those in charge of doing so are famous craftsmen in the field. This type of bow is primarily known not only for its beautiful craftsmanship, but for its smooth draw. Less recurved limbs produce less stress on the string, allowing the shooter to shoot faster and achieve better aim. Therefore, this Asian-type bow was used for both battle and hunting. It should be noted that the bow was made from organic materials, an inference made from the fact that no intact Magyar bow has been recovered from any of the tombs or cemeteries of the Eurasian steppe, which indicates its total biodegradation. However, what has been unearthed almost intact are the bone plates (called *siyahs* or *szarv* in Hungarian) that the ancient Hungarians used to strengthen bow limbs and improve their handling.

The first to elaborate a theory about the use that the Magyar gave to the bone plates was the Hungarian archaeologist Károly C. Sebestyén. Following this discovery, it became clear that the Hungarian bow was actually very similar, if not identical, to the Asian recurve bow. Sebestyén dedicated a large part of his work to trying to recreate this type of arch; however, the lack of literary documents and artistic representations of the time made the work difficult.

The first reconstruction of the bow was carried out by the Hungarian sociologist Fabian Gyula, who had shown a deep interest in the Sebestyén discovery. After a long time of deep research, they concluded that the most effective material for the reconstruction of these bows was maple wood. In addition, he used deer ribs for the reinforcement,

Hungarian gray cow horn for the body, and deer horn for the blade reinforcements. The only difference between his reconstruction and Sebestyén's attempts was that Gyula's bow was less recurved, thus varying the shape of the undrawn string.

Nevertheless, despite the effectiveness of their bow, the Magyar could do nothing against the Mongolians. In 1241, five armies invaded Hungary from the northwest, destroying between 50 and 80 % of the settlements on the Hungarian esplanades. They were the men of Genghis Khan, a warrior and conqueror from what is now Mongolia, who managed to unify all the tribes of Northern Asia under one empire: the Mongolian Empire.

4.2 The Mongolian bow

«An arrow alone can be easily broken, but many arrows together are indestructible».

Gengis Khan.

In the 13th century an empire stretched from Hungary to China. It was the Genghis Khan Empire, a Mongolian prince who managed to unify all the nomadic tribes that lived in the Asian steppe, which became the goal of his life as his own words pointed out: «Within seven years I have succeeded in completing a great work and unifying the entire world into one empire».

The first years of Mongolian imperialism were characterized by periods of internal struggle and the rapid replacement of different dynasties. However, in the 5th century, the Mongolian Empire controlled a vast territory that stretched from Manchuria (China) to the Lake Balkash area, on the border between China, Kazakhstan and Kyrgyzstan.

In the 12th and 13th centuries, the Mongolian army could be considered one of the best in the world thanks to its excellent military strategies and great mobility. Both Genghis Khan and other military leaders managed to implement innovations that made his army not only a feared enemy, but warrior people capable of conquering vast territories and winning battles even when in a minority. The Mongolian tribes were capable of traveling countless kilometers on the back of their horses. Their resistance was not only due to the strength of their animals: the horsemen carried pieces of raw meat under their mounts with which they fed on their marches. But, in addition, they developed a bow and a shooting technique that allowed them to defeat their enemies with little effort.

The Mongolian bow

In the cold Siberian steppe, near Nérchinsk, a Russian city located on the left bank of the Nerch River, there is an inscription carved in stone. It mentions a meeting of Mongolian dignitaries, who had met there after conquering various areas in Sartaul (Mongolia). Specifically, the inscription mentions a character: Esungge, the nephew of Genghis Khan. The reason? It is said that he was able to shoot at a distance of 335 alds (536 meters)… and hit!

The archery tradition of the Mongolians is widely known. Even since ancient times, they have celebrated the Nadaam Festival, a festival that continued after Mongolia gained its independence from China in 1921 thanks to the invasion of the White Russian troops (nationalists) of general Román Ungern von Sternberg, and that has reached our days.

The Nadaam party, which also receives the local name of *erin gurvan naadam*, similar to the Olympic Games, is held throughout the country during the summer holidays, where they compete for three days in the so-called Three Men's Games (this name is maintained although women now also participate): Mongolian wrestling, horse racing and archery. In the discipline of archery, you shoot at targets drawn on leather hoops located at 75 meters (men's category) and 60 meters (women's category). Another game that takes place within this discipline is shooting at 8 cm baskets made from sheep gut, into which the archers shoot 20 arrows per turn.

Mongolian archer

Thanks to these festivities, the Mongolians not only keep their traditions alive, but they can also recall the glory days of their people, a glory they achieved thanks to their mastery in handling their powerful bows (which were able to shoot great distances) and their skills as horsemen. To train in these arts, the Mongolians held quite unique skills competitions, if only because of their difficulty. One of them consisted of shooting at a willow branch lying on the ground and picking up the broken piece without stopping the horse at a gallop. In addition, they organized tournaments throwing clay targets placed on a Ferris wheel that was progressively increasing in speed, also mounted on horseback. All this with an amazing aim.

Mongolian bows were the same as those used by the Magyars, recurved and compound, although with some variation at the end of the blades. In fact, it was more like a perfected version of the Scythian bow, even though it preceded the Mongolian bow by some two thousand years. Mongolian bows were also influenced by the Turkish ones, although they were topped with a piece of hardwood in the shape of a goat's foot, which gave short bows greater power. This innovation meant that the Turkish bow, despite finding no rival among the European crusader troops, could do nothing against the Mongolians and their compound bow. Writer and historian James Chambers describes the Mongolian compound bow thus:

> The bow was the most important weapon of the Mongolians. The English medieval longbow had a draw of 34 kg and a range of up to 229 m, but the smaller bows used by the Mongolians had a draw of between 45-68 kg and a range of more than 320 m. The speed was increased by the difficult technique known as «the Mongolian thumb ring». The rope was tightened with a stone ring worn on the thumb, which released it more quickly than the fingers. A soldier could bend and draw a bow on the saddle by placing one end between his foot and the stirrup, and he could fire it in any direction at full gallop, timing his shot between his horse's steps, so that his aim would not be thrown off when the horse's hooves hit the ground[26].

Two things stand out from Chambers's words. The first is the power and range of the Mongolian bow, a power that has surpassed any record in shooting distance, greater even than modern bows. Although the reason for this power is unknown, it is believed to be due to the way the Mongolian bows were built, as well as the materials used in their manufacture. The Mongolian bow was built with the same quality base as the Chinese one, its direct competitor: horn or bone, melted tendons and glued with a glue made from fish entrails, and wood. Since obtaining these materials depended on the different seasons of the year, the construction of a bow took at least twelve months.

Some authors believe that up to five pieces of wood were used to build the Mongolian bow: one for the central part (the handle of the bow), the two flexible wooden blades, and another two for the ends, made of very hard and resistant wood, to the touch of the rope. Its hard and strongly recurved points gave the string a quicker recovery after shooting the arrows, and allowed the string, once released, to rest on the limbs, the main difference between the Mongolian bow and other Asian compound ones.

---

[26].- Taken from www.lograrco.es

Each horseman carried three bows that he used depending on the distance at which he was going to shoot and the objective to be reached. To ensure that they were never without arrows, they carried three quivers, each containing 30 arrows. And it is that the Mongolians were a cautious people, who even took two or three horses with them in each campaign to always have fresh mounts.

Mongolian arrows were also made of wood, they were heavy and had elaborate forged metal tips. These points were capable of piercing armor, since they were hardened by heating them red hot and cooling them in salt water. In addition, the Mongolians used different arrows depending on the distance of the shot: short arrows with large, broad heads for short distances, and arrows with small heads for long distances, which were much more effective.

But, in addition, Chamber's description highlights the mention of an element that we had not found in any of the archery practices described so far: the thumb ring.

The Mongolian bow and thumb ring

When shooting an arrow, the apache or Mediterranean style is characterized by pulling the string with three fingers, forming an acute angle at the point where the fingers pull the string. In the case of the Mongolian bow, this angle is even more acute, because the archers used a very different technique from that used by European archers: they drew their bows using only the thumb.

The Mongolian archers used the thumb because it is the strongest finger of the hand and it is the one that has the most throw. With this technique, the other fingers were bent and the hand was down, perpendicular to the face, improving the range, power and penetration capacity of the arrow. However, excessive use caused finger injuries or even long-term malformations.

In order to prevent this, **the Mongolians created a thumb ring. Thumb rings were usually made of leather, although different materials, such as jade or other precious stones, could be used.** The leather also used to have an additional tab on the inner side, and was sometimes made with a notch in the center to indicate the archer's optimum draw point.

But the Mongolian soldiers were not just archers and horsemen; In addition, they carried out exploration, guerrilla work... However, what they never did was face the enemy in hand-to-hand combat, but they had to first immobilize them and harass them with their incessant rain of arrows, which turned the Mongolian army into one of the most feared in history.

Genghis Khan's Mongolian army

In addition to the training we have mentioned, the famous Genghis Khan launched the *nerge*, two great annual hunts. In them, animals were driven to deep valleys or precipices; once grouped, Khan shot the first arrow, thus opening the hunting season. The chilling thing about the *nerge* is that their goal was not hunting for food, as the Mongolian warriors subsisted on millet, fermented milk, dried cured meat, and *kuomiss* (fermented mare's milk), and in case of extreme necessity, a hole was opened in the horse's vein to drink its blood. The *nerge* were actually a model for future military campaigns, a form of training.

The bow and horse were more than just training for the Mongolians; they were intrinsic to their nomadic and warrior lifestyle. Even the clothing of the Mongolian warriors served them to carry out a perfect fusion between the mount of their small horses, comparable to the current pony, but with which they were able to cover distances of up to 100 km in a day, and the shot of their arrows. The basic panoply of a Mongolian warrior consisted of:

- Flexible leather boots, half-round or full-round.
- A compound bow.
- The quiver and the arrows.
- The coat, which could also be a lamellar armor.
- A small circular shield.
- A metal helmet.
- A scimitar or Turkish-style sword.
- The mount, also protected by lamellar armor or leather armor reinforced with metal thread.
- The thumb ring.

Similar to what happens today in many modern states, where the population must complete a period of compulsory military service and remain in the military reserve, under the rule of Genghis Khan all men between the ages of 16 and 60 had to be available for war. Thus, the Khan guard went from being made up of 1000 men in 1206 to being made up of 135 000 men in 1227, the date on which the steppe leader died.

These nomads of the Asian steppes were used to hard life and inclement weather, as they formed one with nature and its adversities. In addition, the discipline of the men of Khan was draconian, and any fault, from the most minor such as falling asleep, to those considered more serious, such as disobedience, were punished by death.

Army platoons were organized according to a decimal system:

- 10 men – 1 *arban*.
- 10 *arban* – 1 *jegun* (100 men).
- 10 *jegun* – 1 *minghan* (the basic battle unit, 1000 men).
- 10 *mingham* – 1 *tumen* (10 000 men).
- 2 or 3 *tumen* – 1 army corp.

The Mongolian army entered combat positioned in rows of five *mingham*. Two ranks of cavalry stood in front, and another three light cavalry units stood behind. Between the gaps left by the lines of heavy cavalry were the archers, who fired ceaselessly and made a sweep (*tulughma*) on both flanks of the enemy.

This positioning was done in absolute silence, and they were coordinated by black and white pennants (to imagine how this happened, we can think of the instructions that ground personnel give to airplanes using reflective flags). But suddenly, in the midst of that absolute silence, the *naccara* sounded. These war drums, carried on the backs of camels, burst into the silence of the steppe and gave the starting signal for the attack of the Mongolian warriors. The rumble of drums was followed by shouts, howls, and a hail of arrows.

As with animals during *nerge*, enemies were cornered but given an escape route to flee. Of course, this was nothing more than a trap. In a previous chapter, we talked about how the passage of Thermopylae had been the tomb of the Spartans in front of the Persian troops.

Well, in the case of the Mongolians, the effect was the opposite. The enemies, seeing themselves cornered, avoided the battle and fled. This allowed the Mongolians to chase and massacre them for hundreds of miles and for days, even weeks. They called this technique «the open end tactic».

In addition to this open-ended technique, in his book *Secret History of the Mongolians*, the author, Laureano Ramírez Bellerín, explains fourteen other different strategies used by the Mongolians in battle:

1- Straight soldiers and scattered stars. Divide the Mongolian troops into smaller units to prevent the enemy from encircling the troops so that they could appear unexpectedly in the battle and withdraw just as quickly when it was over.
2- Archers tactics. The archers responded with their arrows to the percussion of the drums. Even though some of them shot from their horses, others got down to fire on foot, protected by small rounded shields. Once the arrows had done their job, the cavalry charged.
3- Cavalry charge. Once the archers had fired a certain number of casualties had been claimed, the Mongolian cavalry charged the enemy simultaneously and from all angles, a strategy that could be repeated in successive charges if necessary. This direct charge into enemy lines was preferred.
4- Provocation of disorder. In order to create confusion among the enemy troops, it was common for the Mongolians to bring oxen or horses with them to the battle lines and even to the fortifications.
5- Tactic of exhaustion. When faced with a strong enemy, Mongolian troops would shoot arrows until the enemy was forced to relocate due to lack of provisions. It was then that they launched the final attack.
6- Confusion and intimidation. One of the most common tactics of the Mongolian troops was to light many fires in their camps, make the horses raise great clouds of dust, and mount women and children on the horses in order to make the enemy believe that there was a greater number of soldiers than they actually had.

7- The simulated withdrawal. Although they are classified separately, simulated withdrawal is basically another technique to create confusion. The Mongolian troops pretended to flee, thus attracting the enemies. Although they believed that they were chasing defeated Mongolians, they were actually tiring their opponents and disuniting the troops, so that they could counter-attack when the situation was more favourable.
8- Attraction in the ambush. Similar to the previous technique, the ambush lure was used primarily in sieges or difficult or narrow terrain. The Mongolians broke through the heavily defended ranks of their enemies by a slow, gradual retreat, and waited for the opportune moment to turn on their followers and strike back.
9- Arch formation tactics. The Mongolians sent out two units of cavalry in arc formation to make sweeps, while a third unit of warriors remained hidden in the center. Thus, the Mongolians were able to attack the enemy from at least three different points.
10- Strategic flanking. On some occasions, Mongolian generals would position a unit in front of the enemy formation. What the opponents did not know was that this unit was merely symbolic, and that the generals had sent cavalry troops through open mountain roads and trails, full of wild animals, to attack the enemy from behind.
11- Surround. Avid strategists, the Mongolians took advantage of their enemies' exposed flanks and defenseless rear areas to distract the enemy, both on the battlefield and in the cities they attacked.
12- Combination of swords and arrows. Whenever possible, Mongolian archers were to avoid close combat. That was what the heavier infantry units were for, who would defeat the enemy definitively once the archers had caused enough damage.
13- Hot pursuit and dispersal tactics. When the Mongolians were victorious in battle, they were ruthless and barbaric; they pursued their enemies in an attempt to annihilate them completely. In case of losing, and if they had to make a retreat, the Mongolians dispersed in the flight trying to avoid being surrounded

and increasing casualties.
14- Bush group tactic. The Mongolian warriors moved in small groups and undercover. This tactic was especially effective at night and in low-light situations, as it prevented warriors from being seen.

These military strategies, the excellence of the compound bow, the ferocity of the warriors and their small horses gave Genghis Khan and his men the most important victories of the time. Not only did they reach Europe, but they were able to stand up to the Chinese, people with a thousand-year-old archery tradition.

4.3 The Chinese bow

«A gentleman must not compete, but if he is forced to, he will compete in archery. Before the competition, the opponents must bow, and after it, drink together. In this way, the competition will have chivalry».

Analects, Confucius.

China is one of the great civilizations of antiquity and treasures thousands of ancient traditions. One of them is archery. And it is that the historical records tell that, more than 2000 years ago, Yang Youji became the first archer of ancient China. His story has reached our days. Yang Youji, an outstanding archer since childhood, decided to take on Pan Hu, another renowned archer. The duel consisted of hitting a target located at a distance of 50 paces. When Pan Hu got it right, the audience went wild. Then it was Yang's turn, who looked around and said, «The target is too close and too big, let me shoot a willow leaf a hundred paces away».

He asked for a willow leaf to be dyed red. He shot. And it was right. Incredulous at what he had seen, Pan Hu stained three more sheets for Yang to fire again. One by one, Yang pierced the three leaves with his arrows, unleashing madness in the audience. Pan Hu was left with no choice but to accept defeat from him.

Two thousand years have passed and Yang Youji's name may have been forgotten, but his legacy continues to inspire many Chinese to constantly improve their job skills. More specifically, **in the field of archery, Yang's story inspired a shooting contest, the Sheliu. This contest is also another example of how in the oldest civilizations the bow and the horse almost always went hand in hand.**

On both sides of a path, rows of willows were placed from which a piece of approximately 30 cm of the bark was torn off to facilitate shooting. Each archer had to tie a handkerchief to a willow branch, and shoot an arrow with the aim of breaking that branch. Next, they had to try to grab the handkerchief from the branch as they galloped past on the back of their horse. Whoever broke the arrow won and was also able to recover the handkerchief. Although it seems simple, they were very difficult skills to coordinate, since sometimes the horse galloped too fast and other times the breeze could move the branches at the most inopportune moment. This contest was one of the main exercises in military training during the Song dynasty (960-1279).

Going back in time, the Chinese knew of the bow long before the exploits of Yang Youji, and China's first bow is believed to have been devised around 4000 years ago. Already in the 6th B.C. the famous philosopher Confucius included archery, one of the six oldest arts, among the essential sciences for human development along with writing, arithmetic and music. Besides being an athletic activity, it was considered a way to improve character and develop a refined personality.

At first, the Chinese used the weapon to hunt, until it ended up becoming an intrinsic part of their culture, on and off the battlefield. This is the reason why community rituals related to archery were developed. Thus, in modern times, the bow and arrow were able to coexist for a long time with firearms, even after during the second half of the Qing dynasty (1644-1911), firearms were little by little imposing themselves as the weapon of choice. When the Chinese began to fight against western powers (England, France, the United States) in the early 19th century, foreign troops suffered heavy casualties at the hands of Chinese archers, accustomed to practicing their aim and flair on moving targets. located in the narrow alleys of Beijing.

However, we cannot specifically speak of a Chinese style when it comes to archery. Throughout history there have been variations and evolutions in archery techniques. For example, during the Han dynasty (206 B.C. - 220 A.D.) there were seven different types of archery manuals, including one written by general Li Guang, known for his battles against the Xiongnu tribes of northern China. During the Ming dynasty (1368-1644), there were fourteen archery schools, each of which published its own technical manual.

These variations, moreover, are supported by archaeological evidence and historical sources. Most varieties of the Chinese bow were compound bows, although longbows and compound bows were also used. Modern reproductions of these bows are inspired by these three types of bow but, in addition to using traditional manufacturing methods and materials such as bone or wood, they currently combine them with modern materials, such as fiberglass, carbon and fiber reinforced plastic.

The main traditional designs used in China are:

- Scythian bow: they were short and curved bows. Archaeological remains of Scythian bows from the time of the Eastern Zou dynasty (770-256 B.C.) have been recovered.
- Longbow: longbows and wooden compound bows were especially popular in southern China, where the humid climate made it difficult to use the curved bow. Remains of a Chinese longbow from the western Han dynasty (475 B.C. - 9 A.D.) with a length of 159 cm, a width of 340 cm, and a thickness of 140 cm have been found.
- Wood compound bows: these types of bows, with a length of between 120 and 150 cm, were ideal for the humid climate in southern China. Based on archaeological remains in the area, it is known that this type of bow was typically made of laminated bamboo or blackberry wood, covered with silk and lacquered to protect them from the weather.
- Long *siyah* compound bows: this type of bow was very popular from the time of the Han dynasty to the end of the Yuan dynasty (206 B.C. - 1368 A.D.). These stiff-pointed compound bows were very similar to Hun bows. At first, these bows were long and thin; however, during the Yuan period the elongated points became thinner but heavier. The *niya, gansu,* and *khotan* bows are examples of this type of bow.

- Compound bows of the Ming dynasty (1368-1644 A.D.): during the Ming dynasty in China, different types of bow coexisted: the *chenzhou* bow with short points bent forward, possibly related to the Korean bow and popular in northern China; the *kaiyuan* bow, a small-medium sized bow with long points that was the weapon of choice for high-ranking officials throughout China; and the long-pointed bow, ideal for shooting on horseback, typical of the north of the country. There was also the taiping people's bow, similar to the Korean one, appreciated throughout China for being an authentic craft work. In addition to the diversity of bows and techniques, it should be noted that all these bows have only been represented in art and literature, but archaeologists have not yet found any original bows from this period.
- Compound bows of the Qing dynasty (1644–1911): the *manchu* bow became popular in China during the reign of the Qing dynasty. Unlike other Asian compound bows, the *manchu* bow was long (up to 170 cm) and had long, heavy points (up to 35 cm in length). This design responded to a need for speed in favor of stability, and has endured to this day. Apparently, this type of bow has influenced Tibetan and Mongolian bows today.

Chinese archer

Despite these design variations and the existence of different schools of archery, they all had one thing in common: the emphasis they placed on archery as not only a physical exercise but also a mental one. This philosophy influenced other people with whom China was in contact over the centuries, such as Japan.

4.4 The Japanese bow

«An arrow, a life».
Kyudo expression.

At the northeastern side of China is Japan, the country of the rising sun. When you think of the Japanese country and its weapons, the first thing that comes to mind is the well-known samurai (servant soldiers). Nevertheless, something that not everybody knows is that the tradition of archery in Japan is also deeply rooted, and displaying this oriental philosophy does not only consist on shooting an arrow: it is a moment of intense meditation for the archer, which takes place in an almost ceremonious way.

Samurai are traditionally associated with swords. Initially, however, the bow was their weapon, since they valued archery as much or more than sword fighting. And with the bow came the horse. In order for the samurai to be able to shoot accurately at individual targets and at close range from their horses, short bows, about 60 cm long, were made from whalebone or horn. On the other hand, the longest bows reached 240 cm, and they were built so that the *ashigaru*, the infantry, could carry out their massive salvos with the maximum possible power.

The *yumi*, the classic Japanese bow, is an asymmetrical bow of great elasticity and power. It is created from a strip of noble wood, such as sumac, and two strips of bamboo. To reinforce the glue, a rattan cover was used, which also served to balance the uneven power of the bow, and was then covered with a waterproof lacquer. The Japanese bow also had a strange design. From the bow hand to its lower point there is much less distance than from the hand to the upper point. This strange design is given by his way of understanding the shooting technique on horseback.

Between the 12th and 16th centuries, Japan was ruled by the *shoguns*, the military leaders. During this long period of time, military schools were created that taught both horseback shooting (*yabusame*) and archery on foot (*kyudo*), the modality that prevails today. Another traditional archery practice that has lasted for 1300 years is *inuomono*, a sporting practice that consisted of shooting dogs with arrows from a horse and in a closed area.

Japanese archer practicing *kyudo* with her traditional *yumi* bow

Beginning the 16th century, and for reasons beyond the scope of this book, the Great Masters of Zen settled in Japan. As the bow ceased to be used as a weapon of war, it became an instrument whose practice contributed to increasing personal development, and acquired a mystical concept by combining Confucian, Buddhist and Shinto beliefs. From the 17th century, *kyudo* acquired an institutional character, and the Great Masters of Zen founded different schools for the teaching of archery, all rivals. Many legends about feats carried out by *kyudo* masters are told from this time; however, there are few ways to guarantee the veracity of these stories, since the schools were characterized by their iron secrecy.

With the schools, a different conceptualization of *kyudo* was also born. The *kyudo* (way of the bow) is seen as a unique combination of mysticism and institutionalism, and perfectly elaborated rituals are developed to take, draw and shoot the bow, which have been maintained to this day.

Archers shoot with a longbow, constructed of bamboo, using techniques developed by old master archers. The arrows are long to try to achieve a flight as straight as possible, without parabolas, from the moment the arrow leaves the bow and hits the target. To throw them, the bowstring is pulled tight until it reaches the back of the shooter's ear, and the archers use a special glove, so valued by them that they passed it down from generation to generation as the best heirloom. The clothing used during this ritual also had its own meaning, as it emulated the outfits worn by archers before the feudal period. Japanese archers wear a shirt or camisole called a *shozoku*, pants (*hakama*), and socks (*tabi*).

When we talk about the mystical nature of archery in Japan, we must point out that it does not necessarily imply that it is religious, but that it is an almost spiritual exercise. The Zen, the thought on which *kyudo* is based is not a philosophy that deals with morality, but it is more related to experimentation than to understanding. Although this is difficult to understand from a western conceptual framework, it serves to explain the concept of Zen and Zen experiences: the important thing in archery is not so much that the arrow hits the target, but the style of the shot, the ritual by which the entire shooting process takes place. Furthermore, the mistake has its own positive aspect, as it allows the archer to learn and grow.

The ritual of the bow is framed within two principles. The first is that «the shot must be as natural as free-flowing water», that is, at the moment of the shot, the spirit, mind and body must be in harmony. The second is that, when shooting, the arrow has to slip between the fingers in the same way that snow slides down the blade that supports it. That is, it must fall naturally, without intentionality, as if it were not a fully conscious process. For this to happen, the Zen principle of «here and now» must be applied to *kyudo*: at the moment of shooting the arrow, the past and the future do not exist, only the moment counts. Each arrow shot must be for personal enjoyment; you shouldn't celebrate successes or despise missed shots, just focus on the arrow. It is also about learning to control emotions so that thought and action occur simultaneously. Being able to forget about the outside world, archers enter a trance-like state.

Although this understanding of *kyudo* seems very different from the western understanding of archery, there are valuable lessons to be learned from the Zen approach. Regardless of where you are in the world, or your individual goal of mastery of the bow, the truth is that mental serenity, mastery of emotions, acceptance of mistakes as a means of learning, concentration... they are all indispensable qualities for any archer.

This brief description of the ritual behind archery in Japan reveals that *yumi*, the word used to designate the bow, does not actually refer to an object; it refers to a discipline of body, mind and spirit, to its symbiosis with the tool (*kyû* or *yumi*) and to the process that leads to that result (*dô* or *michi* in its *kun* reading). Thus, the *dô* is the process by which an individual is capable of reaching self-knowledge, seeking ways to improve as a person during this process. However, to fully understand what *yumi* and *kyudo* are, it is necessary to compile the history of archery in the land of the rising sun.

History of the *kyudo*

As we have already explained, the *yumi* has gone through many stages. It was used as a hunting instrument and as a weapon for more than 5000 years, before becoming a tool for physical and personal development.

Pre-history. From 5000 to 300 B.D.

The history of the bow and arrow in Japan begins in the pre-history. Archaeological sites confirm that the earliest inhabitants of Japan used arrowheads made of stone, as well as tools made of sand to make arrows. The oldest *yumi* ever found is over 6000 years old. Furthermore, excavations report that during the *jômon* period (1400-300 B.C.), the Japanese used the bow primarily as a hunting weapon, an activity that had existed in Japan for nearly ten centuries.

As in other parts of the west, human settlements developed into villages, and these grew into towns. Japanese society also evolved, its politics became more complex and disputes between people became inevitable. Thus, the *yumi* went from being a hunting tool to a weapon of war, a use that lasted from the 7th century B.C. until the unification of Japan in the 11th century A.D. From that moment, it began to give a mystical character; and, in the 12th century A.D., the first archery school was founded in Japan.

It was in pre-history when the *yumi* began to be given ceremonial use. On the one hand, *yabusame* (horseback archery) was used as a way of offering to the gods and Buddha, and had not yet become what it is today, an activity in which an archer mounts sitting on a galloping horse and successively fires three special arrows, tipped in the shape of a turnip, at three wooden targets. Also, occasionally, the palace guards would nod their bows as a reminder that the palaces were guarded by archers.

Ancient Japan. From 300 B.C. to 1000 A.D.

For more than 5000 years, the inhabitants of the islands of Japan developed archery as an instrument for hunting, war, and, little by little, it became a mean of physical and spiritual development.

The Japanese bow is believed to have acquired its particular asymmetric shape (with the grip at 1/3 full length) around 300 B.C. At least, that is indicated by a drawing found in a bronze bell in which the first figure of the bow appears as it is made today, since in previous times it had been built from a single piece of wood. The reason why they were designed this way is not exactly known, and there is only conjecture about it.

One of the possible explanations is that, in the 5th century, Chinese culture was first introduced to Japan. In addition to Confucianism, the Chinese introduced the notion of compound bows, which were made from bamboo and wood. From archaeological evidence showing remains of arrowheads in human skeletons, it is known that during the period known as *yayoi* (from 300 B.C. to 250 A.D.) the Japanese continued to use the bow as a weapon of war. During this period, the use of the bow and horses in battle begins. These knight archers are the ancestors of the samurai.

However, it was the arrival of Confucianism that gave archery its mystical character. The legendary archery master Shotuku Taishi established the first school of archery, the Taishi Ryu School (574-622), which was revived in the feudal period.

Feudal Japan. From 1000 to 1600 (the era of *kyujutsu*)
The feudal era in Japan is a period of legendary wars and it is also the time of the heyday of the samurai. We must remember that, before being known for their mastery with the sword, the samurai were great horse archers, so archery also reached its maximum splendor, mainly due to war needs. Such was the development of archery techniques that, during the Genpei wars[27], 80 % of army casualties were caused by arrow attacks.

As we have already seen, however, archery was itself considered an art (*kyujutsu*). Thus, archery schools (*ryu-ha*) dedicated to the regulated teaching of archery in its different modalities (on foot, on horseback and of a ceremonial or religious nature) began to become popular. These modalities are:

- *Yabusame* or three target shot.
- *Kagasake* or bamboo hat shot.
- *Inoumono* o dog hunting.
- *Oitorigari* or bird hunting.
- *Makigari*, hunting.

27.- The Genpei Wars are a series of civil conflicts that took place in ancient Japan, at the end of the Heian era, between 1180 and 1185, and that pitted the Taira and Minamoto clans against each other. Following the victory of the Minamoto clan and the consequent fall of the Taira, the first *shogunate* (military government) in Japanese history was established in Japan, putting the samurai in political and military command.

Above all, different archery practices were developed on horseback, with bows that had a tension of between 15 and 40 kg.

The first school of archery (*ryu*) was founded in the 12th century by Henmi Kiyomitsu, who created a mounted archery entertainment system known as *henmi-ryu*. Kiyomitsu was followed by Takeda and his school, as well as Ogasawara Nagakiyo with his Ogasawa-ra-ryu. This school is credited with the beginnings and survival of modern *yabusame* techniques.

The devotion to archery as a practice brought with it the emergence of legends that narrate the exploits of the great Japanese archers. It is said that the archer Nasu no Yoichi was able to shoot an arrow from his horse that hit directly on the shield (a fan) of the mast of a Taira boat[28] anchored offshore. The downing of the shield was interpreted as a bad omen for the battle, and the enemy withdrew. Another narrative tells that Minamoto no Yorimasa[29] killed a demon with his sacred bow. This ritual continues to this day in the Shinto and Buddhist traditions.

In the year 1274 the Mongolians invaded Japan, and archery once again becomes the true protagonist, but this time due to a series of reforms that were carried out within the *heiki-ryu* school. **The Japanese bow was unable to meet the precision needs required to defeat the Mongolians. Yoshida Shihemori is said to have transformed the school by implementing the techniques learned from his mentor, Heki Danjō Masatsugu, who introduced a new shooting technique for the on-foot modality that gave greater precision and speed.** Later, Heiki-ryu was divided into different sects, called «ha», among which Sekka-ha stands out[30]. Some of these schools have stood the test of time and continue to exist today.

Another famous sect or branch is the one created by the Buddhist monk Chikurinbo Josei. He founded the Heki-ryu Chikurin sect, which would influence both temple archery (of a mystical nature) and

---

28.- The Taira (now Hira) refer to a hereditary clan from the Hian period (794-1185). With this name, the emperors of the time referred to former members of the imperial family. The Taira clashed with the Minamoto during the Genpei Wars.
29.- Japanese warrior and poet. Samurai of the Minamoto clan (1106-1180).
30.- The Sekka-ha sect adopted a radical way of *kyudo*, based on their deep mystical experiences and influenced by the maxim «nothing is necessary».

Toshiya[31] or Zen, in later stages of *kyudo*.

In 1543 the Portuguese arrived in Japan, and the first Jesuit missionaries with them. Thus, begins a direct commercial and cultural exchange between Japan and the west. This exchange also meant the arrival of firearms to the Japanese country. In 1575 the battle of Nagashino[32] took place, in which, for the first time, the Japanese are aware that arrows and bows had given way to firearms. In this way, the common soldiers of the Japanese army began to use firearms, while the *yumi* was reserved for the highest-ranking samurai.

Although firearms displaced the bow and arrow over time, the *yumi* continued to be the symbol of the fighting spirit for the samurai. It was because of this connection and because of the development of a game called *tôshiya*, explained below, that the tradition of archery could be maintained to this day.

Transition to modernity. (From 1600 to 1867). (The era of *kyudo*)
In the year 1606, a samurai named Asaoka Heibei successively shot 51 arrows from one end to the other of the verandah[33] of the Sanjūsangen-dō temple in Kyoto. In this way, the *tôshiya*, although it had originated in the year 1156, became an official game.

In commemoration of Heibei's deed, archers participating in the *tôshiya* shoot their arrows from the southern end of that verandah to the northern end (about 120 meters). As a target, a kind of exquisitely decorated curtain was placed. The archers competed in four different categories:

- *Hyaku-i* (百射, ひゃくい, lit. *one hundred shots*). The archer who hit the target with the most arrows out of a total of one hundred was declared the winner.

---

[31].- *Toshiya* was an event held as part of *kyujutsu* (the Japanese martial art of shooting at a target with a bow and arrow). It is also known as *dosha* or *domae*. The contest was held in the west wing of the Rengeo-in (also known as Sanjūsangen-dō) temple, with archers shooting their arrows from south to north down a long corridor.

[32].- The battle of Nagashino was a military confrontation that took place in 1575 at Nagashino Castle, in Mikawa province. The castle was besieged by Takeda Katsuyori, a leading samurai of the Takeda clan, for threatening the clan's supply from him. Both Tokugawa Ieyasu, founder and first *shōgun* of the Tokugawa shogunate, and Oda Nobunaga, a famous feudal lord, sent troops to rescue and liberate the castle and Takeda Katsuyori's troops were defeated.

[33].- Covered and closed gallery or balcony, usually with glass.

- *Sen-i* (千射, せんい, lit. *one thousand shots*). The archer who hit the target with the most arrows out of a thousand was declared the winner. In 1827 an 11-year-old boy named Kokura Gishichi hit 995 arrows, shooting from the middle of the verandah.
- *Hiyakazu* (日矢数, ひやかず, lit. *number of arrows per day*). The boys who had not yet celebrated their *Genpuku*[34] could compete in this modality. The archers had to shoot as many arrows as possible in a 12-hour period. In 1774, a 13-year-old boy managed to shoot 11 715 arrows, hitting the bull's-eye with almost every shot.
- *Ōyakazu* (大矢数, おおやかず, lit. *many big arrows*).
  It is said that this modality dates from the *keichō* era. Archers shot as many arrows as possible in a 24-hour period. The record was set by Wasa Daihachiro when, on April 26, 1686, he shot 8133 of 13 053; that is, an average of 544 arrows per hour and 9 arrows per minute.

The names of the champions were hung in the temples, on a certificate that also showed the age, the number of arrows fired and the date of the competition.

From 1606 to 1867, the *yumi* formed much of the samurai's training, both physically and spiritually. And it is that, in 1603, the third and last shogunate, the Tokugawa, was established in Japan. It should be remembered that the shogunate was essentially a military dictatorship, so the samurai, as soldiers, played a very relevant role in society. For example, Ogasawara Heibei Tsuneharu dedicated himself to rescuing the Ogasawara ryu, a school focused on horseback archery, thus creating Yabusame and the modern Ogasawara style practiced in Tokyo today. It is also in this period that the *yugake* (gloves), that are still used today, were developed.

However, in 1867, the *yumi* went through a declining period that coincided with the end of the shogunate and the disqualification of martial arts.

34.- *Genpuku* was a Japanese coming-of-age ceremony, inspired by an ancient Chinese custom, marking the transition from child to adult status and the assumption of adult responsibilities.

Meiji restoration (1867)

As the land of the rising sun modernized, martial arts and schools (*bu jutsu*) lost importance, since they were classified as useless. Surely, had it not been for the efforts of the martial arts masters, transforming their target, perhaps the practices would not have survived.

During the time of war, martial arts were aimed at killing or injuring other people. Individual survival was essential, but eliminating the opponent was the *dô*[35] to achieve the long-awaited individual perfection. However, when firearms displaced the bow and arrow, archery became an optional art for the samurai.

In addition, the last shogunate was followed by a time of stability. Without battles to fight, the samurai were forced to take refuge in the temples and perform administrative tasks; there were those who became artists and philosophers; some even became Buddhist monks. Intellectuals like Miyamoto Musashi, who wrote the *Book of five rings*, appeared. Influenced by religious and philosophical teachings, the ancient samurai introduced Shinto and Buddhist ideas into the field of archery.

The birth of the term *kyudo* (way of the bow) is attributed to Morikawa Kozan, founder of the Yamato-ryu hybrid school. Since 1660 the bow had become a means of spiritual improvement and development; now, it had also become a way to preserve ancient traditions. Despite these efforts, however, the samurai caste and its privileges disappeared in 1868, when the *meiji* modernization and restoration movement began, a succession of events that led to a change in the political and social structure of Japan. This restoration marks the beginning of the modern period in Japan.

Modernity. (From 1890 to the present day)

Concerned about the gradual adoption of western values and the progressive disappearance of their caste, the old samurai gathered in Kyoto to preserve Japanese identity and tradition through the right teaching of *kyudo*. For example, Honda Toshizane, a *kyudo* instructor at the Tokyo Imperial School, reformed the Honda Ryu school and created the foundations of the current mixed style through the formulation of

---

35.- Path, method.

the Honda-ryu style, which combined the ceremonial style of the *kyudo* with combat. Thus originates the *sha-do*, the path of the shot.

However, this revitalization of *kyudo* did not overcome without controversy, as religious and sectarian influences predisposed the new *kyudo* doctrines. Awa Kenzo, student in Honda Toshizane, created his own school influenced not only by mystical experiences of Zen, but also by the maxim «nothing is necessary», from the manuals of the Sekka-ha sect. But this school was actually a religion: the Dai Sha-do Kyo. Although the sect still exists in Japan and his disciples continue to spread his philosophy, the masters of the time called Kenzo a lunatic and strongly criticized him. And it is that, in reality, Kenzo had never received a formal education in the art of Zen.

Despite this, the controversial idea of *kyudo-zen*, so far removed from what the historical *kyudo* was, and the traditional practice of Zen, has been the most widespread in the west. This achievement is mainly due to the work of the German philosopher Eugen Herrigel, who traveled to Japan with the idea of learning more about the ancient doctrine of Zen. His enthusiasm, his inexperience and his difficulties with the language led him to study Zen through *kyudo*, more specifically under the guidance of the eccentric Awa Kenzo. From these experiences came the book *Zen and the art of Japanese archers*, which was translated into most European languages.

Faced with this sacrilege of traditional practices, in 1934 the Association of Martial Virtues of Greater Japan (the Zaidan Hojin Dai-Nippon Butoku Kai) published the *Kyudo yosoku* (important rules of *kyudo*). However, it was the *kyudo* community itself that opposed to these rules, which fell into oblivion. We must add that, at the end of World War II, something unusual happened in the history of Japan.

In 1945 the allied occupation forces (United States, China and the USSR) prohibited *bu-dô*[36] classes. A year later, all other martial arts doctrines were prohibited. In 1946 the National Association of Martial Arts was also dissolved. However, as part of the easing of the policy towards Japan, in November 1949, a year before the Korean war broke out, the Zen Nihon Kyûdô Renmei, the Japan Kyudo Federation, was

---

36.- Term that encompasses the technical knowledge of contemporary martial arts.

founded. Renowned archers from all traditions worked together to create a unified style of teaching and, thus, democratize *kyudo* throughout Japan. Finally, in 1959, the first edition of the *kyudo* manual was published, which regularized the teaching of *kyudo* in Japan.

This also allowed *kyudo* to be taught in a regulated manner throughout the world. These efforts were also joined by those of Kanjuro Shibata. In 1980, this bow maker for the Emperor of Japan founded the Zenkko International Kyudo School in Boulder, Colorado (United States). Today, it includes 25 groups in the United States, Canada, and Europe that practice the Chikurin Temple style, one that has no ranking system, no *dan* (level) exams, no competitions, and where experienced students help the new ones on their way. Due to different ambassadors and media, *kyudo* leaves Japan and a world community is created, which did nothing but grow during the late 20th century.

The International Federation of Kyudo was founded in 2006. In addition to regularizing and standardizing its teaching, it allowed these rules to reach all corners of the planet. Today there are some 500 000 *kyudo* practitioners around the world, and national federations in England, Germany, Portugal, Switzerland, Spain, Italy, Poland, Holland, Norway, Russia, Latin America, the United States and Canada.

Modern *kyudo* unites the ceremonial, technical, spiritual and sporting aspects. This ancient art continues to be a practice that goes beyond the *yumi dô*[37], and it is, in fact, the *dô* of man[38]. This spirituality of archery was transferred to other areas of Asia.

4.5 Other Asian towns

4.5.1 The bow in Korea

In Eastern Asia, between Japan and China, lies the Korean peninsula. Although the peninsula is currently divided into two, the Republic of Korea (southern Korea) and the Democratic People's Republic of Korea (northern Korea), this was not always the case. Both countries

---

37.- The bow's path.
38.- The man's path.

are currently known for the constant escalation and de-escalation of a conflict that has been going on since the end of World War II, when the USSR and the United States liberated the Korean peninsula from Japanese occupation but, in reality, the linguistic and archaeological evidence shows that the rich history they possess is common to both Koreas.

Korea was unified by Emperor Taejo, of the Goryeo dynasty, in 936. During this time, the advances in Korean society were enormous. So much that, centuries before Gutenberg invented the printing press in Europe, the Asian country created the first mobile printing press in the world. With the arrival of the Mongolians in the 13th century, the country became a tributary state, that is, it sent submissions (tributes) to the Mongolians, a situation that lasted until the fall of the Mongolian Empire, when the Goryeo dynasty was replaced by the Joseon dynasty in 1388.

The era of the Joseon dynasty was covered in such isolation that Korea earned the nickname of the hermit kingdom. However, the first two centuries were years of relative stability. In the 14th century, King Sejong the Great created the *hangul* (Korean alphabet), and also increased Confucian influence in the country. Korea's stability and progress made it an object of desire for the Japanese, who annexed the peninsula in 1910.

Despite the invasions suffered throughout its history, Korea always knew how to measure up to its enemies. One of the secret weapons of this small nation's people was their fantastic archery on horseback, a tradition that began many centuries ago and became official in 1471 with the creation of the Great Ritual of Archery, which mixed archery with state rituals. The competition opened with the emperor shooting four arrows while the citizens sang different hymns. Next, it was the common people who competed in different activities, and the emperor gave prizes to the winners.

The Great Ritual of Archery, created to strengthen the ties between the people and their rulers, also intended to highlight the values preached by Confucius, among which courtesy stood out, considered essential for the peaceful coexistence of people. But, in addition, and as a result of this competition, an archer tradition that went beyond the ritual was established. For example, during the Joseon dynasty, a large number of shooting ranges where middle-class people could practice and military exams were held were created.

Nowadays, archery in Korea is a tradition. Moreover, it is surely not unreasonable to affirm that it is the most valued sport in the country. Perhaps that is why Korea is currently one of the world's great powers in competitive archery. Archers have tough training disciplines, and their work is based on perseverance and a spirit of sacrifice. Thus, in international competitions such as the Olympic Games, Korean archers have proven to be practically unbeatable, both in the female and male categories.

Archery in Korea is a highly recognized sport.

4.5.2 The bow in Vietnam

In May of 2020, the American press exploded against the management that President Donald J. Trump was making of the COVID-19 pandemic. The figures spoke for themselves: in just a few months the virus had killed almost 84 000 people, 25 000 more than the deaths caused by the Vietnam War.

The Vietnam War (1955-1975), also known as the Second Indochina War, and baptized in Vietnam as the War of Resistance Against America, was a war fought to prevent the reunification of Vietnam under a communist government. The conflict arose from the First Indochina War (1946-1954), in which French colonial troops fought against the Viet Minh, an alliance between the Indochinese Communist Party and nationalist groups, formed to achieve independence from France. Most of the financing of the French war Effort was provided by the United States.

However, in 1954 the French were defeated and abandoned their Asian colony. At the Geneva Conference, held between April 26 and July 20 of 1954, it was decided to separate Vietnam into two sovereign states (northern Vietnam and southern Vietnam) and to hold a referendum in 1955 in which the Vietnamese would decide their reunification or their definitive separation. But the leaders of the south chose to carry out a coup for fear that the reunification would win.

Thus, northern Vietnam began the infiltration of soldiers in support of the Vietcong, a Marxist-Leninist organization in southern Vietnam and Cambodia with its own army (the People's Liberation Armed Forces of Southern Vietnam - PLAF), to annex southern Vietnam. Therefore, under the Truman doctrine and the Domino Theory (containing the spread of communism), the United States sent resources to southern Vietnam to prevent conquest by the communist north. In 1964, those resources became troops.

Thousands of analysts and experts have asked and answered in thoughtful reports questions such as «what happened so that France, a colonial power, was expelled by an army led by the peasantry?» or «how could the United States, a country that had demonstrated its military supremacy during World War II, fall against that same army?». The answer goes beyond the iron discipline of Ho Chi Min's men, or the inflexible opposition to the United States interference and the implantation of capitalism. **Much of the success of the northern Vietnamese troops was due to the fact that the bow and arrow, which had disappeared in favor of firearms, were once again used as weapons of war in the 20th century.**

We must also take into account the advantage that the Vietnamese had a thorough knowledge of their territory. In Vietnam, 30 % of the land is occupied by lush forests. In the rain forest there are pines, bamboos, plants with large leaves and crops; mangroves surround the branches of the deltas. The Vietnamese insurgent troops hid among this vegetation and, from the thicket, they shot their thin bamboo arrows, poisoned with extracts from the ipoh tree (*Antiaris toxicaria*), a technique they had learned from the *orang asli* people.

In addition, the Vietnamese used incendiary arrows to burn grasslands and cultivated areas near rivers. The goal was not only to eliminate their enemies, but also to prevent them from finding areas in which to set up their military camps. The reeds that the communist troops found in the fields were used to make traps that were stuck in the bodies of North American soldiers when they crossed the populated Vietnamese jungles. Ancient techniques against the owners of the world.

It is striking that, of all the Asian countries, Vietnam is the only one in which archery has not been associated with a mystical component. Whether due to the necessity of the conflict, or because of the ideology of the Viet Cong, the truth is that the most recent use of archery in Vietnam is far removed from what has been given to it in Japan and China. Now, for those interested in the mysticism of archery, you will be happy to know that, although Vietnam is an exception, countries like Tibet or Bhutan have maintained that spirituality and religiosity.

4.5.3 The bow in Tibet

On February 27 of 2009, Tapey, a young Buddhist monk from Kirti monastery, set himself on fire in a market in the city of Ngawa, located in the Chinese province of Sichuan, before the astonished and terrified gaze of merchants and buyers. Two years later, on March 16 of 2011, the also Buddhist monk Rigzin Phuntsog replied the scene in the same market[39]. The reason for his immolation was none other than to protest the Chinese occupation of Tibet.

These types of revolts against the People's Republic of China have been taking place since China occupied Tibet in 1951, a country that

---

39.- Since June 15 of 2012, 38 Buddhist monks and nuns have been counted who have immolated themselves in the same way in China.

had been ruled as an independent monarchy since 1912. In addition to the immolations, there were also revolts in 1959 and 2008.

Over the years, the Central Tibetan Administration (CAT), the government in exile, has changed its priorities regarding Tibet's self-determination. The CAT has opted for cooperation to ensure autonomy to the point of requesting absolute independence, even requesting «genuine autonomy for all Tibetans living in the three traditional provinces of Tibet within the framework of the People's Republic of China». However, not all exiled Tibetans agree with these positions, and, in 2008, they expressed their frustration through pro-independence revolts.

Although most of the protests were peaceful, there were cases in which they turned into violent proposals. Therefore, the protesters did not have the support of the Dalai Lama, the spiritual leader of the Buddhists. And it is that the teachings of Buddha prohibit the resolution of conflicts through violence; in fact, Ahimsa, an ancient Hindu precept of non-violence and meaning «do not hurt», is one of the main virtues of Buddhism.

This, however, does not imply that the Tibetans do not have weapons or that they do not use them. By tradition, Tibetans are hunters. More specifically, the Kampas, who live on the northern slopes of the Himalayas (in southern China), became famous for the way in which their powerful bows felled wild beasts such as the fearsome snow leopards, and they also served to defend their territories from other enemies.

The bow also has a religious significance. Kurukula, a female Buddhist deity (*dakini*), is depicted as a fierce-looking red figure, with her two pairs of arms shoots a flowery bow to the left; and, with her left leg, she steps on a person. Kurukula is credited with the power to subjugate gods, people and animals, she is invoked as a remedy against snake poison and also to attract love. However, she is also associated with a spiritual function: keeping the fundamentals of Buddhism. Kurukula is the winner of obstacles and helps to achieve enlightenment and the triumph of Dharma, correct pious conduct.

The deity Kurukula, in fact, is not associated with violence. Moreover, the *Kurukullākalpa*, a manual dedicated to the ritual of the goddess Kurukula, reads as follows:

Those who take pleasure in
killing sentient beings
will not succeed in this discipline.
Those who delight in the ten virtues
and possess a unified mind in their devotion to the Great Vehicle,
they will, hereby, in accordance with the words of Vajradharma,
experience supreme realization.

Tibet is not the only country where the deity Kurukula is worshiped. The neighboring country, Bhutan, is a Buddhist country, where archery is also associated with the gods, and the powers of the Kurukula bow and arrows are invoked.

Representation of Kurukula

4.5.4 The bow in Bhutan

There was once a man who was wounded by a poisoned arrow. His relatives and friends wanted to get him a doctor, but the sick man refused, saying that he first wanted to know the name of the man who had injured him, the caste to which he belonged and his place of origin. He also wanted to know if this man was tall, strong, had a light or dark complexion and also wanted to know what type of bow he had shot him with, and if the bowstring was made of bamboo, hemp or silk. He said that he wanted to know if the feather of the arrow came from a falcon, a vulture or a peacock... And wondering if the bow that had been used to shoot him was a common bow, a curved one or an oleander bow and all similar type of information, the man died without knowing the answers.[40]

It is said that, with this story, Buddha tried to teach an impatient student that intelligence when separating the important from the expendable can mean the difference between overcoming a difficulty or being overcome by it. This Buddhist teaching is also one of the tricks of mindfulness that invite us to live in the moment.

In addition to Tibet, another country where the majority of the population follows Buddhism and its principles is the kingdom of Bhutan, known as the happiest country in the world after King Jigme Singye Wangchuck proposed the gross national happiness (GNH) or the gross domestic happiness (GDI) indexes in 1972 as indicators to measure the quality of life of citizens, and as a response to constant criticism of economic poverty in their country, an agricultural country. Located in southern China, on the other side of the Himalayas, Bhutan was born in the 8th century, when the Tibetans expanded their territory and introduced Buddhism. After a period of wars, territorial unification, and after being part of the British East India Company and the British Raj, Bhutan became independent from India in 1949.

In 1971 Bhutan became part of the United Nations Organization (UNO) and it was at that time that archery was declared a national

---

40.- Taken from lucerorodriguezg.wordpress.com

sport. The love for archery in this country is shared by all social classes, from the monarchs to people. Today, competitions are held; and, among these, traditional Mongolian bows are used to launch arrows with a large parabola, so that they hit a target barely 30 centimeters high, located more than a meter high and about 120 meters away, so sometimes it is not easy for the archers to know that they have hit. They count on the public for this: when the arrow hits the target, those present, who are closest to the target, celebrate it by singing and dancing.

This celebration has an almost ritual character. However, this is not surprising, since archery is associated with the gods; and the arrow has mystical connotations and it is associated with prayer and meditation. In other words, it has little to do with other people for whom archery is the basis of their subsistence.

Traditional Bhutan archer

4.5.5 The bow in Northern Asia and Siberia

Previously, we have talked about the Mongolians, their empire and the power of their bow. Today, their heirs still inhabit the inhospitable steppes of eastern Siberia. To survive, they follow the traditions of their ancestors, including hunting. And, additional to firearms, they use the bow.

Today's bows, an evolution of the Mongolian bows and those form northern China, are made from flexible bones on the inside; the external part of the blades, more powerful and resistant to use, is made from glued tendons. The ends are designed so that the vegetation of the forests does not interfere with the shot and the inhabitants of the steppe can continue hunting all the species that live there.

After reviewing the Asian continent and its people, it is time to ask ourselves: what about America?, what is the importance of the bow and arrow throughout History in the American continent?, how did it change with the Discovery? In the next chapter, we address these interesting questions.

CHAPTER V

THE BOW IN THE AMERICAN CONTINENT

About 110 000 years ago, the last Ice Age began on the Earth. The planet cooled to such an extent that even the tropics were affected. The water of the seas and oceans also froze, and concentrated on the continents. As the sea level decreased, stretches of land emerged at various points on the planet, connecting independent areas. For example, Australia connected with New Guinea and Tasmania, some islands in the Philippines connected with others in Indonesia, and they also connected the Canary Islands of Lanzarote and Fuerteventura.

The last Ice Age ended around 10 000 B.C. About 40 000 years ago, the receding waters revealed a 1500-kilometer-wide expanse connecting Siberia and Alaska: Beringia, the area now known as the Bering Strait. Some 15 000 years later, hunters from Northeastern Asia crossed over to the Americas, thus beginning human occupation of the continent.

Little is known about the first settlers of the American continent. It is known that they were hunters, but the mechanism they used to obtain food is unknown. In fact, the first evidence that exists regarding the use of archery among this population is, at most, between 2500 and 3000 years old, and the oldest are those found on the Atlantic coast of

North America. The first settlers of the American continent expanded from north to south, using only their simple bows, with non-recurve blades. In a few thousand years, they reached from Alaska to the southernmost tip of the continent. As they occupied it, their societies also evolved. This way, the people that marked the history of the continent were born, such as the Incas; and complex societies developed, such as the Mayans and the Aztecs, with cities, architecture, writing and calendar systems that had nothing to envy the Europeans, who would arrive for the first time in 1492.

5.1 The bow and arrow in the pre-columbian America

The tension could be cut with a knife. The crew of the Santa María, the Pinta and the Niña had left the port of Palos de la Frontera on August 3 of 1492, with the intention of reaching the Indies from the west. It was October, and they had not even sighted Japan, which was believed to be between 3000 and 5000 kilometers away. The harsh conditions of the trip and the smell of rotting food did not help to calm things down.

—Land in sight! —shouted one of La Niña's crew. It was October 12 of 1492, and Columbus and his men believed they had sighted the Indies. What they did not know was that, in fact, they had arrived on the island of Guanahaní, in the Bahamas. They baptized the territory as San Salvador.

The inhabitants of the island of Guanahaní could not ignore the fact that strange artifacts of an almost supernatural nature were approaching their shores, floating on the waves. They were piloted by other strange beings, human in appearance, but very different from the men and women who watched the spectacle in astonishment. They seemed to have come from heaven, they wore strange clothes, they did not have painted faces, they had pale skin, short stature, and their hair was not straight and black. Upon touching land, the visitors offered them unknown objects: colored caps, bells, mirrors, glass necklaces... The natives were amazed at these contraptions. As a symbol of thanks, they offered the newcomers parrots and food.

Columbus and the rest of the sailors were fascinated to see these men and women. Both them and their customs and way of life were nothing like what they knew of Europe, nor what Marco Polo had told of his travels. It was as if these peaceful fishermen and peasants were still stuck in pre-history. They dedicated themselves to the cultivation of plants, many of them unknown to Europeans, such as yucca, and they plowed the land with pointed sticks; they fished with nets and baskets; they lived in huts with roofs made of palm fronds; and the only weapon they knew was the assegai, a small throwing spear topped with an animal tusk or fishbone. Like the Europeans in the Neolithic, the natives did not know iron, much less the weapons carried by outsiders. In the words of Columbus himself: «They do not carry weapons nor do they know them, because I showed them swords and they took them by the edge, they cut themselves ignorantly. They don't have any iron».

Native American hunting with an assegai

Columbus returned to the American continent on three subsequent occasions. However, he died not knowing that he had not arrived to India, but that he had come into contact with unknown people and civilizations in Europe. It was not until Americo Vespucci, a Florentine merchant, explorer and cosmographer naturalized Castilian in 1505, published his work *Mundus Novus* (New World) in 1503, that Europe realized that the Indies of Columbus were, in fact, a new continent. Columbus also died without knowing that the islands he arrived to on his voyages were only the gateway to a vast continental territory, populated by empires and civilizations that had nothing to envy a Europe that had just entered the Renaissance.

5.1.1 Central American people

Teotihuacan, City of the Sun, is the name given to what was one of the largest pre-hispanic cities in Mesoamerica. It is the region where the Teotihuacanos settled and developed, one of the most important civilizations of the pre-hispanic era. Teotihuacan is translated as «place where men become gods, place where gods were made, or city of gods».

The largest monument in the city is the Pyramid of the Sun, whose use is unknown. It is sixty-three meters high, and at its peak was a ceremonial temple. It was built using adobe bricks, covered with stucco and decorated with religious paintings. Legend has it that this is where the sun and the moon originated and, of course, given the nature of this book, the bow and arrow also play an important role in this story.

Being the gods gathered in Teotihuacan, they began to plan the new day. To prepare it, they had fueled a fire that had burned for four years. The divinities Tonacatecuhtli and Xiuhtecuhtli summoned Nanahuatl, who suffered from a skin disease, and told him that from that moment on, heaven and earth would be in his care. On the other hand, the rain gods, Tlalocantecuhtli and Nappatecuhtli, cited one named Nahui Tecpatl. Both candidates fasted and mortified themselves. The offerings of Nahui Tecpatl were lavish, those of Nanáhuatl were meritorious and frugal. Finally, they jumped into the fire. Nanahuatl fell into the flames, and Nahui Tecpatl into the ashes. Nanahuatl ascended to heaven converted into the Sun. There, the supreme divinities, Tonacatecuhtli and his wife, seated him on a throne of pink feathers and tied his head with a red ribbon. However, Nanahuatl remained motionless for four days. Confused, the gods asked what was the reason for his lack of movement.

—I demand the death of all gods —he answered.

Faced with this threat, Tlahuizcalpantecuhtli, god of frost, drew his bow and shot his arrows at the newly crowned sun god. He did not calculate the power of Nanahuatl, who killed him in a sudden way. After him, he killed the rest of the gods of Teotihuacan.

In pre-columbian mythology, more specifically in Mesoamerica, the bow and arrow play a very important role. An attack with arrows not only sentenced the gods of Teotihuacán, but also helped a character named Dzahuindanda or Yacoyooy, nicknamed «the Sun Arrower», to defeat their highest lord. There are several versions of the legend, but the result is always the same: thanks to their arrows, the first Mixtecs managed to occupy Mixteca, the cultural, economic and political zone shared by the Mexican states of Puebla, Guerrero and Oaxaca.

The Sun Arrower was born from the Apoala tree, the being from which the first Mixtecs were also born. According to the chronicles collected by the first Dominicans who arrived in the area, the Arrower left the sacred valley of Achiutla, where the first Mixtecs had settled, in search of a new home for his people. He thus arrived at the Mixteca, which was then uninhabited. Only the sun inhabited that land, so Dzahuindanda recognized the lord of that area in the star. Wanting to settle in those lands, Dzahuindanda challenged the sun in combat; the winner would obtain the right to inhabit the territories. The sun attacked his opponent with his rays, but this one, a daring archer, fired incessantly until the sun turned red, dyed the sunset blood red, and disappeared over the horizon.

Beyond the legends, it is true that in the area of present-day Mexico there were people who were great archers, such as the Olmecs and the Nahuatls. However, to further explain the importance of the bow and arrow in pre-columbian cultures and the role they played as Native Americans tried to repel European conquest, this section describes how the Mayans and Aztecs, the most prominent civilizations of pre-columbian Central America, used this tool.

The Mayan civilization

When the Spanish conquistadors set sail for Central America in 1517, their goal was to subdue the Mayans, a civilization that had developed in southeastern Mexico (in the present states of Yucatan, Campeche,

Quintana, Roo, Chiapas, and Tabasco), occupying practically all of Guatemala and also in Belize, the western part of Honduras and El Salvador, covering more than 300 000 km².

Around 1050 A.D. the Mayans had left the interior regions of Mexico, where their ancestors had prospered, and had gone towards the Caribbean coast in search of other sources of water, such as the lakes and sinkholes of the area. The Mayans, like all great civilizations, relied heavily on crops for their economic power and to sustain their huge workforce. We must not forget that the pyramids that stand out today in Guatemala, Belize, El Salvador and western Honduras were built by Mayan labor, many more than 3000 years ago.

The climate records, obtained from the analysis of formations in the caves, show that, during that time, the Mayan area had received relatively high rainfall, something that benefited the maintenance of the complex agricultural system that they had developed, based on fields, permanent raised beds, paratas, intensive horticulture, forest gardens and fallow land. However, these same records indicate that around 820 A.D. the region was devastated by 95 years of intermittent droughts, some of which lasted for decades and affected the entire empire, which gradually fell apart. Thus, when the Spanish landed, the political and economic power that erected the iconic pyramids of the region and that at the same time had given sustenance to a population of two million people, had practically disappeared.

For two millennia, this Mesoamerican civilization stood out for its great sociocultural development. They established a hieroglyphic writing system (one of the few pre-columbian writing systems that was fully developed), and were also noted for their art, their rich mythology, their number systems, and their knowledge of astrology, mathematics and ecology.

However, the subsistence of the Mayans was not based only on agriculture; the Mayans were also hunters. The *atlatl*, a stick about half a meter long and with a notched end to hold a dart or a javelin, was introduced to the Mayan culture through Teotihuacan in the Early Classic. As we have seen in previous chapters, this stick allowed the missile to be launched with more force and precision than if it were launched with the arm. Commoners also used blowguns. The stone points recovered in Aguateca indicate that darts and spears were the main weapons of the Mayan warrior until the Postclassic period (950-1540 A.D.), when the bow and arrow were fully adopted for both war as for hunting.

Although the Mayan empire had almost disappeared, the Spanish found themselves with some excellent warriors dressed in armor made of cotton and hardened using salt water –with results quite similar to those of European steel armor– and who carried wooden or leather shields, decorated with feathers and animal skins. To defend themselves, they used a sword of great size and weight, made from strong wood and sharp obsidian blades. This is how Bernal Díaz del Castillo describes it, present in the expansion through Mexico:

«Many squads of Indians came along the coast [...], with their cotton weapons that reached their knees, bows and arrows, and spears and shields, and swords that seem two-handed, and slingshots and stones».

This weapon was very similar to the macuahuitl of the Aztecs, another great pre-columbian civilization that occupied Central Mesoamerica from 1325 to 1521.

The Aztec Empire

While the Mayans established their culture in southeastern Mexico, Guatemala, Belize, Honduras, and El Salvador, another people, the Aztecs, more properly the Mexicas, occupied central Mexico and the Gulf area. Although it is true that they coexisted, both people did not reach their peak in the same periods, nor did they focus their existence in the same way.

The first Mayan cities were founded around 750 B. C. (at the same time that Rome was founded) and the last ones were abandoned by the year 950 A.D., when Europe was in the Middle Ages. For their part, the Aztecs founded their empire in the 14th century, when the Medici became the most powerful family in Europe. Their domain lasted barely a hundred years, since the empire fell apart in 1521, with the arrival of the Spanish. In short, the Aztecs reached their peak period 400 years later than the Mayans.

The Mayans made great cultural contributions for posterity. In this sense, the Aztecs also developed important technologies for agriculture, including canals to irrigate crops and drainage systems that left the Spanish very impressed: unlike the Europeans, the Aztecs, even the warriors and conquerors, stood out for their great personal hygiene.

This development of the Aztecs was visible above all in their urban centers. The most important of these cities, Tenochtitlan, was born in 1325 on the shores of Lake Texcoco, where the Mexicas had settled. From there, the supreme leader, Huey Tlatoani, demanded tribute from the conquered people in the form of skins, crops, handicrafts... and even young people for human sacrifices that were offered to the gods. One of the best known Tlatoani was Moctezuma Ilhuicamina, who was elected sovereign of the Mexica state after the death of his uncle Itzcoatl in 1440.

Thanks to his powerful alliances with the *altépetl* (political and cultural entities) of Texcoco and Tlacopan, Moctezuma Ilhuicamina began an expansionist era and extended his domains to the areas we know today as Guerrero, Hidalgo, Puebla, Oaxaca and part of Veracruz. He thus came to dominate the entire Anahuac plateau. Besides, he organized a tribute system that allowed Tenochtitlan to become a very powerful city. But, for those who are interested in archery, what most attracts the attention of the emperor is his nickname. Moctezuma Ilhuicamina was known as «the Sky Arrower», a nickname he earned after spending a sleepless night, alone with his tempered bow, to avoid a possible Tlaxcalan invasion until reinforcements arrived.

We do not know how much truth there is in this anecdote. What we do know is that the Aztecs were excellent warriors. Weapons like the *atlatl* became a true nightmare for the Spanish. The chronicles also speak of the destructive power of the *macuahuitl*, capable of cutting off the head of a nag with a single cut. The same thing happened with the skill of archers when shooting arrows designed so that they could not be extracted from the flesh. Pedro de Alvarado confirmed that he was crippled after one of them hit his leg while he was fighting against the Aztec warriors.

The Aztec bow was made from a combination of hard woods, almost always ash, oak or other woods from the south. They were small in size, barely 150 centimeters, and combined the characteristics of the English longbow and the American flatbow.

The most elaborate bows were treated with oil to protect them from the elements and, in addition, they were laminated with a hard but softer wood that was glued on top and then left to dry in the sun for days to acquire its characteristic hardness and flexibility. **These were the battle bows, used by the warriors, which were also characterized by being decorated with allegorical paintings. On the other hand, there were the hunting bows, which the commoners also had, and which had a much simpler elaboration: it was a simple bow, formed by a piece of rectified hard wood so that the bow bent perfectly, and reinforced with ties to protect it.**

Aztec archer

Since the Aztecs were warrior people, the war bow was the most common. The rope was made up of strips of leather, generally made from a very tight weave of ixtle or wet feline intestines, knotted and dried in the sun so that they would harden without losing their flexibility. For its part, the material used for the manufacture of the arrows was usually maple or ash wood, although the most appreciated were the cane arrows. The points were made of very hard wood, burned, or obsidian. The combat arrows were also decorated with wild turkey feathers.

It is worth noting the special care with which the Aztec artisans manufactured and finished off their arrows, which were also a symbol. The bow and arrow were so important in the life of the extinct Aztecs that the first gift a child received at birth was his quiver with three arrows and a small ceremonial bow. It was believed that the life or death of the newborn would depend on this gift.

The Aztecs had such mastery of the bow and arrow that they managed to defeat the troops of Hernán Cortés in 1520 in the Battle of the Sad Night. Such was the humiliation of the Spaniards that, once the conquest of the territory was completed, a royal proclamation was imposed prohibiting the natives from possessing any article that could be used as a weapon against the Spaniards. This led to the almost complete disappearance of the bow in both Mexico and South America. However, there were two reasons that saved it from extinction.

The first is that the first expeditions to the north of New Spain were carried out by armies made up of soldiers, volunteers and ex-convicts who, before fighting, preferred to make pacts with all the tribes they encountered. The second is that the bow was saved due to the fact that most remote people continued to use it as a means of subsistence, including South America.

5.1.2 The bow and arrow in South America

The traditional image of the bow and arrow in South America is the enormous bows that were held with the feet and shot with both hands, lying on their backs on the ground, to hunt monkeys in the tops of the great trees or birds in flight.

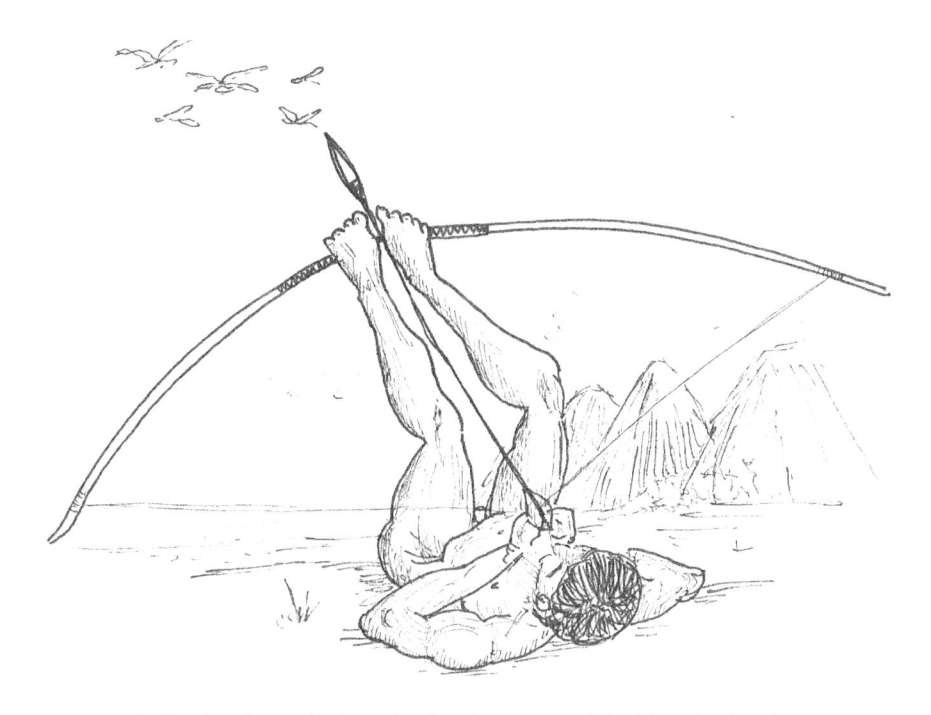

Indian hunting with a bow in what is now part of the Brazilian jungle

However, this is still just a stereotype: the types of bow and arrow are as diverse as the people who inhabited the area, even long before the arrival of Europeans. From the jungle areas of Brazil, the deserts of Peru, and the territories that today are Argentina, Chile and Uruguay, the bow was a common element, although its construction and use depended a lot on the environment in which different people lived.

The bow in Peru: the Incas

«This land is where Nono told me that an Indian woman lived, an Indian woman who lived in the shack and who was killed.
They grabbed her to make her prey but she wouldn't let herself be dominated and they never could because she was very angry because they had killed her husband. So, well, they killed her, they killed her, they threw some dogs at her and then they killed her...

you know that the Indians also killed people and had many arrows, they fell on houses and fucked people up, of course they didn't go away. But in the end they started getting in, they started getting in and the Indians started leaving, leaving.

Now one does not hear about Indians anywhere, right?».

Tachira Museum, Ayacucho, Teófilo Ramírez
(talking bout the European conquest of the area).

Long before the arrival of Europeans in what is now Peru, the bow and arrow had already appeared in its territory. In the Ayacucho region, for example, there are petroglyphs with archery scenes dating back to 600 A.D. It is believed that they belong to the Huari (*wari*) civilization, people that flourished in the central zone of the Andes between the 7th and 13th centuries. Using stone axes, metal clubs, bows and arrows, they conquered neighboring towns and came to expand from the current Peruvian departments of Lambayeque to the north, Moquegua to the south, and even the jungle department of Cuzco to the east.

Two centuries later, in 1438, the Inca Empire was established, the largest empire in pre-columbian times, with Pachacutec as the first Inca, the theocratic monarch. In 1530, the Inca empire occupied an area of 2 500 000 km^2 and ruled over ten million people; it had expanded through the current territories corresponding to the southwestern extreme of Colombia on the border, passing through western Ecuador, Peru, western Bolivia, the northern half of Chile and the north, northwest and west of Argentina. In 1532, the newly crowned Inca Atahualpa met in Cajamarca with the Spanish conquistadors led by Francisco Pizarro. In this meeting, Atahualpa and his entourage were ambushed, the Inca was taken prisoner by the Spanish and executed on July 26 of 1533.

The legacy of the Inca empire is as wide as its territorial extension. His legacy includes words that are still used today: *field, tent, corn, potato* and *vicuña* (a small camelid similar to alpaca and llama), among others. In all the territories that they conquered in different wars, the Incas brought their cult of the sun, their advances in medicine and agriculture, and their mathematical knowledge.

As it was the case with the absolutist monarchies of Europe and with monarchs such as Louis XVI, called the Sun King, the Incas also believed that their rulers were of divine origin and that they came from the sun, which they called *inti* in Quechua. As a general rule, the sun was represented as a large golden disc surrounded by rays. The temples dedicated to him and to his worship were completely covered in gold, such as the Koricancha or golden courtyard in the city of Cuzco. In this same city, the Festival of the Sun (*inti raymi* in Quechua) is celebrated annually, even today, every June 24. The Inca civilization also believed that corn was the tears of the sun due to the golden color of the grains when dried. Thus, one of the main offerings to the *inti* was *chicha*, a drink made from corn.

In Spain, the large cornfields are very typical in the area of Galicia and the Cantabrian coast. This is because corn, native to Central America, grows best in humid climates with mild temperatures. How did the Inca empire manage to grow corn in the Andean zone, overcoming the rugged terrain and inclement weather? The secret was in the development of agriculture techniques, like the stepped terraces, that allowed organizing the cultivation of various products, both from the coast, mountains and jungle. These allowed not only the cultivation of corn, but also some seventy different species of vegetables, such as potatoes, sweet potatoes, chilies (peppers), cotton, tomatoes, peanuts, ibia and quinoa.

These plants also helped develop both medicine and trade within the Inca territory. In fact, *coca* and *chicha* were used as anesthetics in surgical procedures. The Inca healers adopted knowledge from other cultures, such as the Paraca, to develop their knowledge of surgery. In addition to knowing the bandages and perfecting the metal to the point of creating knives such as the *tumi*, specific for medical procedures, they came to perform cranial trepanations to remove pieces of bone or weapons that could have remained embedded in the skull after a military confrontation.

The Incas also made sure that food and resources were distributed throughout the empire. The Tahuantinsuyo road network, in Quechua *qhapaq ñan* or *inka naani* (road of the king or the powerful), connected the important cities of the coast and the mountains, facilitating exchange and communication between different people. Thus, the Incas managed to build an effective means of political-administrative, socio-economic and cultural integration.

Much of this exchange was based on trade. In this sense, the Inca administrators had a sophisticated mathematical system that allowed them to keep accounts effectively: the *quipus* and the *yupana*. The *quipus* were mnemonic systems that consisted of knotted strips. The *quipu* consists of a main rope, without knots, from which others hang (called hanging ropes) of different shapes, sizes, colors and with different knots. Contemporary specialists assure that the colors are identified with the sectors; the shape of the braiding indicates the objects; and the knots, the quantity. There were strips that had no knots, from which it follows that the Incas had conceptualized the number zero. These accounts that the *quipu* showed were actually an accounting system, since the mathematical operations were carried out with the *yupana*, a kind of abacus.

However, accounting was not the only area in which the Incas applied their mathematical knowledge. Architectural constructions such as Machu Picchu and the city of Cuzco demonstrate knowledge in architecture, while the Inca calendar (360 days a year, divided into 12 months, 30 days each month) demonstrates mathematical knowledge in the field of astrology. In fact, some chroniclers claim that the Incas were able to predict eclipses.

Despite this socioeconomic and cultural development, we must not forget that the Incas were also warriors. In addition to the soldiers and traditional weapons that made up the armies, the Inca Empire had an elite corps of warriors who used the bow and arrow as their main weapon. The bows and arrows were provided by the Ashaninca people, an Amazonian ethnic group that still inhabits the jungle areas of Peru and Brazil, and the Machiguenga, an ethnic group that still inhabits parts of the Peruvian Amazon in southeastern Peru. Both towns managed to repel the settlers who came into contact with the Inca Empire, thus preserving their native languages, customs and bows and arrows.

The bows and arrows that the Ashaninca and Machiguenga made for the select group of the Inca army were between 120 and 150 centimeters, and were made with strips of chonta wood, a tree of the palm family that grows in the mountains, in the tropical and subtropical zones of Latin America. The arrows, on the other

hand, were made of lighter materials, such as reeds, long-stemmed gramineous plants that grow mainly near water. Although bronze axes have been found in ancient Ashaninca sites, the arrowheads were rarely made of iron, but instead used bones, pieces of burned and hardened guayacan tree, and even flint.

There are not many chronicles about the use of the bow and arrow by the Incas. The only news that we have date back from the 16th century, which narrates the battles between natives and Spaniards. The references of Pedro Pizarro stand out, who says that, in the siege of Cuzco, they were attacked with arrows, or that Gabriel de Rojas «was shot in the nose with an arrow that entered his palate».

The legacy of the Incas continues to this day. However, despite their might, they were unable to repel the European settlers. The same did not happen with other pre-columbian people, who, although less developed socioeconomically speaking, were able to defend themselves and maintain their customs and traditions to this day.

The Guarani bow

In 2012, in South Korea, the sixth World Archery Festival took place, in which more than 30 countries participated. The victory went to a display of native bows and arrows from various towns in Paraguay, which convinced the jury. These native people are the Guarani, *chiriguanos* in Quechua, or *Tupi Guarani* in their native language, a group of native South American people located in Paraguay, northeastern and northwestern Argentina, southern and southwestern Brazil, and southeastern Bolivia.

Little is known about the origin of the Guarani. It is believed that they are descendants of people from the Caribbean area, more specifically from the mouth of the Amazon River, who migrated south in search of land suitable for cultivation. Thus, they reached the basins of the upper Paraná, upper Uruguay and the southern borders of the Brazilian highlands. Some 700 years later, around the 12th century, they finally reached the territories where these tribes, who share the same linguistic family, are found today. Upon the arrival of the Europeans (16th century), the Guarani occupied the vast forests between the Paraná, Miranda, Tiete, Uruguay rivers, and their tributaries, as well as large stretches of the southern coast of Brazil. For this reason, they were the first natives to come into contact with the Spanish and the Portuguese, for example, Álvar Núñez Cabeza de Vaca, a Spanish conqueror who explored the southern coast of the United States, from Florida through Alabama, Mississippi and Louisiana, and that entered Texas, New Mexico, Arizona and northern Mexico until reaching the Gulf of California, territories that were annexed to the Spanish Empire within the viceroyalty of New Spain.

Guarani archers

Like other nomadic people, the first Guarani were also warriors and hunters. **It is true that the Guarani today are not warriors, but they are still hunters. They use bows and arrows that they make using the knowledge of their ancestors. The bows of the first Guarani were between 2 and 2,5 meters long; they were made of palm wood and lined partially or entirely with interlocking strips of tree bark. The arrows used were made of cane; the tips, made of wood, had different shapes (with teeth, harpoon type, top-shaped) depending on whether the arrows were going to be used for fishing, hunting birds or shooting down a larger game.**

Despite their rudimentary weapons and their simple way of life, the Guarani managed to survive the conquest by the Europeans. They were not the only ones. The territory that today is Chile, Argentina and Uruguay was populated by tribes that have managed to preserve their way of life despite conquests, wars and persecution. One of the most famous of these people are the Mapuche.

The bow and arrow in Tierra del Fuego

Legend has it that, at the beginning of times, the creator god Kooch felt so overwhelmed by his lonely existence in the dark that he began to cry inconsolably. He cried for so long that his tears created Arrok, the main sea. Realizing what had happened, the god sighed. Thus was born Xoshem, the wind, who separated the waters from the mainland. But Koock could not see his creation clearly until he shattered the darkness, giving rise to Xaleshen, the sun; so that the nights would not be so dark, he created Keenguenkon, the woman-moon, who soon became an evil and powerful being. Xaleshen y Keenguenkon fell in love and they spawned Karr, the first star of the day, who was gifted mastery of the tides.

This is how Patagonia and its oceans arose, one in the east and the other in the west. In the latter, Koock established an island for giants and other creatures to inhabit, such as animal-men. One of those giants, Nosithej, kidnapped the mouse-woman and they had Elal together. Upon discovering the pregnancy, Nosithej, furious, murdered his wife and attempted to devour the fetus. At that moment, the ground roared and Nosithej was disoriented. Taking advantage of the moment of fright, Terrguer, Elal's grandmother field mouse, rescued the newborn and hid him in her cave.

Elal grew up very fast and soon became a being of great physical strength. Upon reaching maturity, he challenged his father to avenge his mother. The bitter battle ended with the death of Nosithej and the liberation of all the animal-men from the tyranny of the giants. After this, Elal decided to leave the island. He got on Kookne, his swan friend, and flew off. Thousands of other birds accompanied them on their journey, towards dawn, until they reached Patagonia, and descended on the top of Cerro Chaltén. From the top of Chaltén, Elal saw a desert land and decided to turn one of the flocks that had escorted him into the first men, the Tehuelches. He then created the rest of the living beings. Elal also taught men to hunt, creating the bow and arrows.

With this legend, the Tehuelches not only explained their worldview, but also gave the bow and arrow the origin of their sustenance, a quasi-divine origin. **The truth is that it is estimated that the bow and arrow were present in the Patagonia area 2200 years ago, when the Tehuelches inhabited the Tierra del Fuego area.**

The Tehuelche people were made up of different tribes, who had different customs and ways of life depending on the territory they inhabited. For example, the Selknam, also called Onas, were a Tehuelche tribe that lived in the north and center of the big island of Tierra del Fuego, in Argentina and Chile, until the beginning of the 20th century, and they were excellent archers. Their small bow was made of ñire (Antarctic beech), *lenga* (southern beech) or *maitén* (a native tree to extra-tropical South America) wood, and the arrows were made of *calafate* wood (an evergreen bush typical of Patagonia) and *cauquén* (Patagonian bustard) feathers, with stone points.

Another Tehuelche tribe that inhabited the valleys of the Chilean mountain range and to the east of the Andes mountain range were the Puelches. According to the chronicles of the Spanish conqueror and poet Álvarez de Toledo, they were excellent archers, and their arrows posed a problem for the Spanish who crossed into the western part of the Andes mountain range of Chile. What the Spanish did not know was that, before they arrived, arrows were not only used to fight but were used to send messages. For example, in case of uprising or war, the revolted tribe sent a messenger with a small arrow to another tribe. If the other tribe accepted it, it was an indication that they were joining the uprising.

Upon arriving in these lands, the Spanish not only realized the archery skills that the Tehuelches had, but also observed that they had developed a commercial system that allowed exchange with other people in the area. More specifically, the first Jesuit priests were attracted by the fairs, through which the Tehuelches exchanged products with another indigenous people that still exist today in Argentina and Chile: the Mapuches.

The Mapuches, despite having a linguistic and cultural unity, were also divided into zones: the Picunches to the north, the Mapuches in the center, and the Huiliches to the south. Little by little, they occupied all zones in Chile, until they absorbed or dominated the scattered Tehuelche tribes. It is not well known how the Tehuelches came to be on the brink of extinction as a tribe. Some theories affirm that the Mapuches committed a genocide against the true natives; other voices affirm that what took place was a mapuchization of the Tehuelches.

The debate is complex. However, what is known is that the Mapuche and the Tehuelche, although they had a different language and culture, shared certain survival techniques. One of them was the use of the bow and arrow, which the Mapuches called *chemfelwe* or *chufülwe*. For the Mapuche, on the other hand, the bow and arrow were also a kind of martial art: the education of the warriors was only completed through an almost ritual archery exercise called *pülkitun*.

Most of the Mapuches built their bows with *colihue*, a kind of bamboo cane, made of solid wood, very flexible and resistant. The ropes were made with long and fine strands of kneaded leather, intestines and/or animal nerves, all intertwined to form a cord. On the other hand, they also used *colihue* for the arrows, but choosing thinner and straighter branches. The information we have about the arrowheads comes mainly from the archaeological remains of the Patagonian deserts thanks to which it has been known that they made arrows of different sizes: they measured between 50 and 90 millimeters long, between 12 and 20 wide, and between 3 and 9 thick. The tips found so far are also very diverse. Triangular points have been found, with a straight or curved base; there are arrows with stalks in the shape of a snake; some had perfectly symmetrical edges, other arrows had jagged edges; there were also some with sharp edges, and with ridges on the front part to facilitate penetration.

As for the materials, they were carved in bone or in different types of stone. The stone varied depending on the territory occupied by the tribe. For example, coastal tribes used materials such as veined leucite, reddish aventurite, sardonyx, milky or clear quartz, flint, matte or shiny volcanic glass, and, in some cases, a semi-precious stone such as amethyst. Was there anything more valuable than staying alive in battle or hunting an animal to eat? For their part, the hill and plains tribes stocked up on materials they found on the banks of rivers, such as flint; and on the flanks of elevations, such as quartz, basalt and flint. To tie them to the pole, which used to measure about 80 centimeters, they used fine braided cords made of *guanaco* skin (an animal from the same family as llamas). For the rudders, they used long, narrow parrot feathers, which not only gave the arrow stability, but also a splash of color.

Traditionally, the Mapuche used the bow and arrow to hunt and fish. They were excellent marksmen, hitting targets at a distance of a hundred meters. Therefore, they also used them as weapons of war. However, in combat, these arrows became even more deadly, as they were bathed in a poison prepared from plants and other naturally toxic substances. Thus, when the Spanish conqueror and later governor of Chile, Francisco de Villagra Velázquez, crossed the Andes through the Villarica pass in 1553 and reached the Negro River, he was attacked by the Mapuche. The result? The poison of the natives ended the lives of many of his men.

After 1650, however, no more chronicles are found that mention the Tehuelche or the Mapuche using the bow and arrow. And it is that San Martín tells that, with the arrival of the Spaniards, the Patagonians (so called by the settlers, due to their great size and physical strength), the Tehuelches, adopted the recently imported horse; converted into extraordinary horsemen; they supplanted the bow and arrow by the two or three-stone *boleadoras* and the spear. Thus, these people became invincible until the arrival of the armies of general Julio Argentino Roca in 1870 and his conquest of the Patagonian Desert.

Actually, this change from bow and arrow to spears and boleas with the arrival of the horse is somewhat atypical. As we have seen so far, many people throughout history had favored the use of the bow and arrow on horseback, and many of them had perfected both techniques to the point where they became nearly invincible warriors and built vast empires. The same thing happened with the natives of North America, who, on horseback, increased and perfected the bow for hunting and war.

5.1.3 The bow and arrow in North America

Around 12 000 years ago, centuries before Columbus and his ships reached what are now the Bahamas, the ancestors of the so-called «Native Americans» crossed from Asia to what today is known as Alaska. When Europeans arrived in the New World in the 15th century, an estimated 50 million people inhabited the entire continent; 10 million of them in the area that is now the United States and Canada. The diversity of these people was such that anthropologists and geographers studying the first inhabitants of the American continent, and more specifically the northern part of the continent, divided the area into cultural zones: Arctic, sub-Arctic, northeast, southeast, Plains, Great Basin, California, Northwest Coast, and Plateau.

This division gives us an idea of the cultural wealth of those European settlers designated as «savages», a term that later served to justify the displacement of these people and their exile to reserves that still exist today. However, for this section, we are not going to refer to these geographical and cultural divisions, since detailing in depth the customs of all these people, even if only in relation to the bow and arrow, almost requires a book itself. Therefore, this section will limit itself to the most commonly known tribes and exploring how people as diverse as the Eskimos and those who inhabited the area of Florida or the deserts of the southern United States used the bow and arrow for their survival, the types of bows that they made, the materials with which they made these tools and how they used them.

It is worth starting with the Arctic zone. This choice is not trivial, since the Inuit (Eskimos) were not people who generally used the bow and arrow. It must be taken into account that the main source of subsistence for these people were seals and cetaceans, and that piercing the thick layers of fat of these animals with a simple arrow is practically impossible. Instead, harpoons were used made from wood that was collected during the thaw season and treated with animal fat to protect it from the cold winters; the harpoon tips were made of bone. However, the archaeological remains found in the area of Greenland and British Columbia show that arrowheads were used in these areas. For example, in the Haida tribe, bows with wide and very flat blades were used for this purpose. This is because, depending on the animal species that inhabited the area, the first Eskimos also fed on bears or caribou, whose skin was easier to pierce. This type of arrow is very similar to the one that current Eskimos use today.

There is linguistic, archaeological, and historical evidence that prove that some of the Eskimos migrated from present-day Canada between 1500 B.C. and 1100 A.D. These gathering and hunting people were divided into two tribes: the Navajo, who settled in the Colorado Plateau; and the Apache, who came to inhabit the Rio Grande basin. Apache hunters used common, short and simple bows, which they made from the flexible branches of native trees, such as cedars, cypresses or wild olive trees. These same branches were used to create the arrows, which were short, with tips usually made of stone or metal. The Navajos, for their part, built simple bows out of pine or spruce wood, with a few turns of string every two or four inches on the limbs to reinforce the bow. The arrows were also short, but had metal tips and long feather quills to give them stability.

The Navajos are one of the largest native people in North America, but the Ojibwa were also of great importance. This town inhabited the present Canadian zone of Ontario and the present American zone of Wisconsin and Minnesota. The Chippewa, also hunters, built short bows, shooting small arrows tipped with bone or shell. These shells came from the coastal area, indicating that there was already a vast trading system established throughout the continent before the arrival of the Europeans.

In the same area of Wisconsin, although more towards what are now the states of Ohio and Michigan, the Huron Indians, also known as Wyandot, had settled. They lived in small communities of up to

1000 individuals, in well-fortified villages, and inside which they built houses of up to 60 meters. The main resource of the Huron was the harvest of corn, beans and squash, supplemented in part by hunting and fishing. To carry out this activity they used longbows, similar to the English one, and they carried the arrows on the waist fastened with a rope.

Also, in the northern and central United States lived the Arapaho, also called «people of the bison», occupying the eastern Great Plains (currently Colorado and Wyoming). The Arapaho sided with the Sioux tribe and were strong allies of the Cheyenne. These last, who called themselves Xa-ii-la, «the human beings», crossed the Missouri River at the same time as the Crow and Lakota people.

Native American

The Cheyenne and the Crow engaged in a bitter struggle for territory. The first, though avid warriors, lost their sacred bow to the second. Although they were simple bows, made to shoot short arrows, the bow was considered sacred because it was the symbol that united them as and was a fundamental element for their worldview, just like the famous sacred pipe of the Lakota (more commonly known as the peace pipe). The survival of the Cheyenne depended on the recovery of this bow. The Lakota played a fundamental role in this story, since they were the ones who managed to recover it from Crow territory and return it to the Cheyenne, with whom they forged a strong alliance from that moment on.

The arrows used by the Cheyenne were similar to those of the Navajo, with long tips and long feather-decorated shafts. However, the bows were somewhat flatter. Those who also had flat bows, although short, were the Karcuk. This tribe, which inhabited the California area, used animal skins as quivers to carry arrows, usually from a coyote or prairie dog. They also used to carry another crossed arrow in their mouths.

Farther west, in the area that is now California, there were also a large number of tribes who used the bow and arrow as a hunting tool and as a weapon of war. Examples for this are the warriors of the Hupa tribe. Culturally, the Hupa were a mix between the Nootka and the Kwakiutl of the northwestern part of the continent, and the Californian tribes of the southwestern part. More specifically, they were very similar to the Yurok and the Karok, with whom they had an excellent commercial –thanks to canoes made of sequoia wood, they exchanged food from the interior; salt fish, molluscs and algae– and cultural relationship, as they often married each other or held joint ceremonies. The Hupa were excellent basket makers, they knew agriculture and used wood. They were great hunters, but before the arrival of the settlers they fed only on roots, fruits, salmon and deer. To hunt them, they used a flat bow, reinforced with ligatures on the blades and richly decorated. The points had a slight recurve and the arrows, unlike other tribes we have talked about so far, were long, with flint points and long feathered rudders.

The Wintu, inhabitants of the Sacramento Valley area, also used short, flat bows, although slightly curved, and tipped with flint to shoot their long arrows. However, the existence of this town was not recorded until 1826, when settler Jedediah Smith arrived in Wintu territory. The arrival of the white man meant an almost total annihilation of the Wintu. Between 1830 and 1833, almost 75 % of them died from a malaria epidemic. Survivors faced the loss of their livelihoods as settlers' sheep and cattle destroyed the tribe's reservations. In addition, the mining activity led to many of the natives being enslaved in the gold mines, while the waste from the mining activity polluted the rivers from which they drank.

This area of the Sacramento Valley was also inhabited by the Maidu, people known for their skills as basket makers, despite not knowing the textile techniques of their neighbors. The Maidu lived by collecting fruits and seeds; fishing for salmon and eels; and hunting bears, deer, rabbits, ducks, fallow deer, and geese. To hunt them, they used short bows with the points curved inwards. To make the ropes, they used vegetable fibers and obsidian for the tips of the arrows.

The Pomoan also lived in California, more specifically in Sonoma county. These people were originally from the San Francisco area. The Pomoan built bows for hunting and war, and depending on the activity they were intended for, they could be short or long. Nevertheless, the arrows were always built long, made of sharpened wood, including the tip. Unlike other Native Americans, the Pomoan were not confined to a reservation. Even before the arrival of the colonists, they lived in small groups without a central political structure, and their economy was based on hunting and gathering and they did not practice agriculture. It was probably this semi-nomadic lifestyle that helped them survive.

As we advanced at the beginning of this section, the list of archer towns is very extensive, and covering it all would give us enough information for another book. However, this list gives us a fairly accurate picture of how arrow making and use also varied according to indigenous traditions and cultures. From defensive use, to hunting to provide food and clothing, these beautiful bows were necessary and were manufactured throughout the North American subcontinent, from the plains and steppes to the most arid deserts, where skins were also used. of snake to decorate the bows and protect them from humidity. Even the natives of the Antilles, among whom the Karibes stand out, used the bow to hunt, fish and defend themselves against attacks by other tribes and later by the conquerors.

Modern times

The rise of the bow in North America, however, came in modern times, when the Europeans, and more specifically the Spanish, introduced horses. When one thinks of Native Americans, one often imagines them mounted on the backs of mighty horses, galloping up to giant bison to shoot their arrows at close range. Well, that image has its origin in the European conquest. Despite the power of the horse, the bow they used was too short and weak to bring down an animal the size of bison, and that is why they had to get so close to them. In fact, equines were so successful that many tribes ended up organizing hunting championships on horseback, even in jungle areas.

The horse was also a great ally of the Native Americans during the time of the conquest of the west. They used the bow and the horse to defend their territories. However, they could do little against the pistols and rifles of the newcomers. In the second half of the 19th century, native people, their customs and traditions, their culture and their gods, as well as their bows and arrows, were in decline.

When it comes to the bow alone, though, it wasn't all bad. Upon arrival, the Europeans became interested in the use that the natives made of the bow and contributed to their own knowledge about its construction and preservation. This helped to maintain the interest on this legendary weapon on the subcontinent.

In 1828 the first archers club was created in the new continent, specifically in the city of Philadelphia. It was called United Bowmen. But it was after the Civil War in the United States (1861-1865) when the use of archery was promoted.

At the end of the war, the states of the Union prohibited the Confederates from using firearms. Therefore, the brothers Will and Maurice Thompson moved to live with the natives of Florida and decided to learn all the techniques related to the art of the bow and arrow. Maurice wrote a book called *The witchery of archery* and thus helped to increase national interest in the sport. The result? In 1879 the National Association of Archers was created, which was in charge of organizing competitions at a national level. The enthusiasm created caused the National Hunting Shooting Association to appear in 1939, an association that continues to exist today.

The same thing happened around the whole world. The bow and arrow were being displaced over time by firearms, which have greater range and allow greater lethality with little effort. However, those who really admired the art of the bow and arrow, those who understood that these two simple and, at the same time, immense objects are part of our history as a civilization, have always done everything possible to preserve this ancient tradition.

In the next chapter we explore precisely what the fruits of these efforts are. Without going any further, archery has remained a hunting tradition in many areas of the planet, from the Amazon to recreational hunting in western countries, and has even become an Olympic sport. If anyone thought that time was going to end this discipline, they were wrong. The bow and arrow are more alive than ever.

CHAPTER VI

THE BOW IN THE MODERN AND CONTEMPORARY AGES

« The good archer is not judged by his arrows, but for his aim».

Thomas Fuller, historian and member of the Church of England.

With the advent of firearms, the bow and arrow gradually disappeared. As we have seen in each chapter so far, the fall of the great empires of history, the colonization of distant territories and the progressive modernization of war techniques made that traditional weapons, including the bow and arrow, were gradually replaced by weapons of greater power, precision and lethality. However, some nostalgic people did not want to let archery fall into oblivion.

In Chapter 3, in the section that talks about the bow in England, it was mentioned how at the end of the 18th century, in the midst of the ecstasy of the Victorian Era, an unusual fervor for archery was awakened. Exclusive archery clubs became a popular meeting point for members of high society, and gradually spread throughout the country. In addition to the already mentioned Royal Toxophilite Society, some of the most famous were the Royal Kentish Bowmen, Woodmen of Arden and Royal Company of Archers. Their existence lasted for the next century and some have even survived to this day. Such was the popularity of the bow that these clubs even reached the American colonies. In 1787 the Royal British Bowmen was created, an American national society where uniformed archers practiced their marksmanship and made themselves known in society.

It is striking that the term *royal* precedes the name of most of these societies, which owes its explanation to the support given to them by King George IV (1762–1830), even when he was still a prince. The future monarch was an accomplished archer, and was appointed President of the Royal Kentish Bowmen, which enabled him to take on the Royal Company of Archers as an unofficial honorary guard for his visits to Scotland. It was him who standardized the rules of the competition, which until then were different in each club.

The first to adopt these standards in 1754 were the Finsbury Archers. The new system is none other than the one that remains today, the classic dartboard with concentric rings: a yellow one in the center (although, as a curiosity, it should be noted that at the time it was golden, decorated with authentic gold paint), followed by a red one, a white one (which was eventually changed to blue), a black one, and a blank outer one.

The prince also unified the distances, 100, 80 and 60 yards (91,44, 73,15 and 54,86 meters, respectively). It is true that when one thinks of an English longbow, the first image that comes to mind is a siege or a pitched battle from the Middle Ages, and it is even possible that it is also associated with hunting. Regardless of the image that each one evokes, they are always activities traditionally associated with men. However, the abundant number of photos and paintings from the late 19th and early 20th centuries depicting female archers is striking. It is true that archery was basically a male activity, but gradually women made their way until their participation was accepted, at first, to end up being their gender the predominant one. The factors that led to it were several.

6.1 Women and the «renaissance» of the archery

There are those who think that it was also the English monarchy that played a fundamental role when women took the leap to the fore in the field of archery, popularizing this activity. Although not as active as

George IV, his successors, William IV (1830-1837) and Queen Victoria (1837-1901), continued to support the archery tradition. More specifically, Victoria became quite interested in this sport and also practiced it, which contributed significantly to the good image of women archers and their acceptance in a society as strict and corseted as the British one.

In 1834 the queen agreed to patronize The Society of St. Leonards Archers, a society founded by the three Mackay sisters. In 1837, shortly after her coronation, the queen renamed it The Queen's St. Leonards Archers. Thanks to the work of the sisters and the donation of the land by James Burton, the society set up the Archery Ground, some impressive gardens for archery practice.

However, long before Queen Victoria was able to go public with her support for archery, it was already a deep-rooted practice not only in British high society, but also among women. How, when and why did this change occur?

Woman of the time practicing archery

This question is much more pertinent if one takes into account that, as a consequence of the Napoleonic Wars (1803-1815), and due to the demand for soldiers from the front, archery declined and only the most popular clubs and tournaments barely survived. Although the war raged, the practices of the end of the previous century provided the basis for a rapid revival of archery.

In addition to archery treatises written by enthusiasts, the surviving clubs facilitated access to new archers and encouraged the transmission of knowledge from earlier centuries. With the exception of Scotland, traditional bow building had been virtually lost, but new builders soon appeared in England who relearned and/or rediscovered the techniques of the previous century. In this process there was something that changed: from 1820 many of the clubs and societies began to admit women among their members.

No single convincing reason has been found to explain why it happened, but we are going to analyze some of the circumstances that led to it.

First of all, the practice itself had changed. It should be remembered that it was King George IV who unified the rules, and that archery was no longer about shooting into the air to try to get as far as possible, but about shooting accurately at a target. This trade-off from accuracy to range led to the need for less powerful bows, making archery a much more accessible and engaging sport.

In addition, the connoisseurs of the time highlighted the health benefits of this sport. For example, Horace Ford, in his *Archery: its theory and practice* (1859), highlights the benefits for the body and mind of practicing this exercise, especially outdoors. As he describes it, the physical and mental benefits make it similar, according to those studies, to current yoga.

Maurice Thompson's *The witchery of archery* (1879), whom we have mentioned when discussing the bow in America, devotes an entire chapter to explaining why archery is an acceptable practice for women and how practicing it for good does not interfere with their feminine condition, including the fact that it is a sport that can be done with the ostentatious dresses of the time. Moreover, he even compares it to cricket, another popular sport among the English elites, assuring that this, due to the type of movements it requires, can harm women due to the use of corsets, something that does not happen when practicing shooting with bow.

Indeed, the presence of women archers was not due to an issue of gender equality; on the contrary, very marked gender roles continued to exist. But, on the other hand, the activities in which women could participate were very limited, so it is not surprising that they took advantage of any opportunity to get out of the house and participate in social activities.

The fact that the archery clubs were mixed made attendance an extraordinary opportunity to facilitate contact, exchange and relationships between the different sexes. The breaks between runs were the perfect opportunity for attendees to enjoy the outdoors and chat. This is shown by the paintings of the time, which reflect shooting club scenes in which there are men and women talking around tables placed near the shooting line by the servants, who also served food and drink. Therefore, it does not seem surprising that many parents pushed their daughters to participate in this type of event with the aim of presenting them in society, nor that many marriages were forged between arrows and targets.

This is also reflected in the novel *Daniel Deronda*, written and published in 1876 and under the male pseudonym of George Elliot, by the writer Mary Anne Evans. Her book, like others by the same author, is characterized by its realism, its moralizing component and its scathing satire of the English society of the time. In it, the protagonist goes to the Grand National Archery Meeting (the meeting of the Great National Archery Society) with only one idea in mind: to dazzle everyone present and look for a husband among the gentlemen, for which she tries to choose the most suitable dress. The novel presents the reality of this competition as a great marriage market, which was very similar to what happened in real life.

Therefore, it is not surprising that, as a result of these marriages between arrows, the hobby was passed on to sons and daughters, thus continuing the love for archery and its legacy.

The Grand National Archery Meeting (GNAM) that Evans talks about in his novel is precisely the product of the great (and growing) popularity of archery at this time. The number of clubs and societies, as well as the demand for bows and the number of builders to satisfy it grew. *The archer's register*, a book published in 1864, reports that by mid-century there were 146 archery societies in England and Wales, 22 in Ireland, and 9 in Scotland, each with between 100 and 200 members. Given this popularity, in 1844 William Gray took the initiative to create the GNAM, an annual archery tournament based on the rules imposed by King George IV in the previous century.

Seventy-four archers participated in the first meeting of the GNAM, but it was not until the second that a female category of participants was admitted. The fact that eleven women signed up was considered a success. And, although in the immediately subsequent calls the registered number did not reach ten, in the 1950's the proportions between men and women began to balance out, in a percentage of around 90/70. Despite this parity in numbers, gender differences continued to exist; without going any further, the participants did not even use the same type of bow.

Male bows were purely functional. Women's, on the other hand, had a careful aesthetic, being able to have silk grips, pearl arrow-rests and ends to hold the rope made of elaborately carved horn. Regardless of the gender of the bow owners, the manufacturing process was lengthy. It could take between five and six years, since the wood and the adhesives had to dry between phases, and the construction process was very careful. Walnut wood, yew wood (generally imported from the Spanish Pyrenees, due to its high quality) and even exotic woods such as lancewood, a New Zealand tree, were used. This reflects how, effectively, archery was a hobby only available to members of the highest social classes.

Generally, bows were built in one piece or two layers, laminated, carved and sanded to a shape with a D-shaped cross-section (although there were elliptical ones as well). The blades were two separate pieces that were glued down the center in a fishtail-shaped joint to achieve the largest possible joining surface. Its power was around 50 pounds (22,68 kg) for men and 30 pounds (13,61 kg) for women, not so different from the current one and enough for the distances between 70 and 100 yards at which men shot (around 65 and 90 meters) and the 50 and 60 yards (about 45 and 55 meters) at which women shot.

Gradually, the popularity of archery spread to the working classes as well. Public arcades were opened and tournaments independent of those of the upper classes began. But, in addition, the national tournaments were opened to any participant, regardless of their social class, and the names of archers who were not affiliated to any club or society began to appear in the participation registers. In the cases of the humblest classes, the bows were much more modest, although they fulfilled their purpose. For those who could not afford to buy a bow, some cities offered the possibility of renting them for a small sum.

This popularization of the bow allowed this tradition to be preserved well into the 20th century, even surviving the two world wars and the arrival of other outdoor sports, which offered a greater variety of leisure activities.

6.2 The bow in the 20th century: two world wars, the interwar period and the Olympic Games

Starting in 1874, sports such as tennis began to be very successful in England. Not only were they added to the offer of outdoor sports that you could choose from, but they were also mixed. Therefore, although archery continued to be one of the most popular sports, the number of archers and the total number of clubs were reduced from 100 to 68.

However, between the end of the 19th century and the beginning of the 20th century, archery began to gain more and more strength in continental Europe. France, Belgium, Switzerland, Sweden, the Netherlands and Germany, whose archery federation, the Deutscher Schuetzenbund, was founded in 1861, join the list of countries that are beginning to practice it. Thanks to the improvement of means of transportation and communications, international competitions can begin to be organized. The first of these was Le Touquet, held in France in the summer of 1900, in which English, French, Belgian and Swiss archers participated. Its success was such that in subsequent years several more editions were repeated, until in 1914 the competition was suspended after the outbreak of the First World War.

However, the most famous of all sporting events was the Olympic Games, which in modern times were first held in Athens in 1896. The first edition of the Games was exclusively for men. In the words of its organizer, the French, Pierre de Coubertin, the inclusion of women would be «unskillful, uninteresting, aesthetic and incorrect». This mattered little to the Greek Stamata Revithi, who ran the marathon on her own a day after the men did, although she was not allowed to enter the stadium and her mark was never officially registered.

In Paris Games of 1900 the situation changed. For the first time, women were officially allowed to participate, and 975 men and 22 women competed. Swiss Hélène de Pourtalès was the first woman to win Olympic gold, in the 1 to 2 ton sailing category, as part of a crew of three: her, her husband and her nephew, since sailing was a mixed category. The first Olympic champion in the women's individual category was the English Charlotte Cooper. She won in the singles tennis category, although she also won an Olympic title in the mixed doubles later on.

It was in this second edition that archery made its debut as an Olympic sport. However, despite the fact that it was a sport that had become popular among men and women, these Games only had a men's category, in which 129 French, 18 Belgians and 6 Dutch participated. It is worth to mention that, despite the popularity of archery in the United Kingdom, archers of that nationality did not participate in such edition. This is because the Olympic Games did not yet enjoy the current prestige and, to the British's eyes, their national tournaments, which were also held that year, had more weight.

The third edition of the Olympics was in 1904, and was held in Saint Louis (United States). Although the long and expensive trip meant that only American archers participated, it was also the edition in which the women's archery category premiered. Twenty-three men and six women participated, and Matilda Howell was the first Olympic champion of this sport, winning gold in the two individual categories and in the team category. It is worth noting that Howell, who was a 17-time US National Champion, became interested in the bow after reading the articles and comments of the aforementioned Maurice Thompson.

Archery participated in the Olympic Games of San Luis in 1904

In its fourth edition (1908) the Olympics returned to Europe, more specifically to London. But, for this occasion, archery was not an excessively popular sport either: 41 English, 15 French and 1 American participated. However, regarding the English athletes, it stands out that it was the first time in which more women (25) than men (16) participated. The winner was the English Queenie Newall, gold in the only women's category. This victory earned her the still-standing record of being the oldest woman to win an Olympic medal, aged 53.

Newall entered archery late, in 1905, and won four regional tournaments before the Olympics. But, in addition to her skills as an archer, Queenie Newall's victory was propitiated by a strange coincidence. The Olympic winner had a serious competitor in one of the UK's best archers, Alice Legh. Legh was a national champion 23 times, and she had been a national champion no more and no less than 18 times when she was invited to the Olympics. However, for reasons that remain unclear even to this day, she declined the invitation and instead sent Queenie Newall, her protégé. After the Olympics, Newall only managed to take the title from Legh three times.

The First World War brought a break in national and international competitions, as well as in the activities of archery clubs and societies. But, in addition, there were a series of changes in the world of archery that would have been unthinkable a decade before: men went to the front, suffering numerous casualties, and archery became dominated by women, so in 1922 the records of the clubs showed a ratio of 10 women registered for each man.

On the other hand, the conditions of equality experienced by the men at the front meant that the class barriers that had existed up to that time were also gradually disappearing. Although archery remained a sport for the rich, many clubs and societies began to open their doors to citizens of other social classes, although it could be debated whether it was really done out of conviction or the need for survival.

In any case, the 1920's saw a slow return to normality in the sport. During this time also appears an important specialized magazine, Archery News, edited by a woman, Christina Philips. The 1930's, meanwhile, brought with it a growing interest in competitive archery and many technological innovations regarding the bow. In 1931, the archery federations of Czechoslovakia, France, Hungary, Italy, Poland, Sweden, and the United States founded the International Archery Federation (FITA) with the aim of coordinating international competitions and bringing archery back into the mainstream. be an Olympic sport. The Federation was adding countries until reaching the 153 that it brings together today.

Also, the new materials developed by the industry in the interwar period and the increase of scientific studies on the physics of the bow allowed great technological advances in the world of archery. The

A WALK THROUGH ITS HISTORY

bow, which had changed little throughout history, was perfected. Sweden and Germany tested bows made of new materials, such as steel, and sights became popular to aim and increase precision against instinctive shooting. In addition, Clarence Hickman and Paul Klopsteg, American physicists and engineers, experimented with the physics of the bow and arrow. Thanks to their discoveries, the bows went from having a D-shape, inefficient for storing energy, to having recurved and flat blades with a laminated composition, which is the prevailing shape today.

Although the Second World War caused another slowdown in the world of archery, the advances of the 1930's, both technically and competitively, continued until the sport developed into its current form. Today archery is not only a highly competitive sport, nor has it been reduced to the practice of hunting, but rather it has become a recreational sport enjoyed by thousands of men and women around the world, regardless their physical or social condition.

6.2.1 Archery at the Paralympic Games

The Paralympic Games, created for the participation of people with different abilities, emerged as a rehabilitation exercise. More specifically, it was Dr. Ludwig Guttman, a prominent Jewish neurologist, who was a refugee from the German Nazis, who established a rehabilitation schedule for World War II veterans suffering from spinal injuries who were in the Stoke Mandeville Hospital, in the British town of Aylesbury.

For these injured, who had been diagnosed as permanently disabled, the fact of being able to compete, although initially it was only against each other, was key in their rehabilitation process. Such was the success of this therapy, both physically and emotionally, that very soon Stoke Mandeville Hospital began organizing national competitions against other hospitals and clubs. The first of these coincided with the opening day of the London Olympics (1948). Just twelve years later, in 1960, the first Paralympic Games were held in Rome, Italy. Thirty-two years later, Antonio Rebollo, a Spanish Paralympic athlete, launched the arrow that lit the 92nd Barcelona'sOlympic and

Paralympic flame, lighting up the world of sport and putting archery in the foreground.

The website paralímpicos.es clarifies the circumstances in which these athletes participate. Paralympic archery has the same rules, distances and procedures as the competitions at the Olympic Games. Athletes stand at a distance of 30, 50, 60, 70 or 90 meters, depending on the category, and shoot arrows as close as possible to the center of a target that measures 122 centimeters in diameter. The Paralympics program includes individual and team compound and recurve bow events, both in men's and women's categories, and can be performed in wheelchair or standing modalities.

Archers are divided into three categories. The Open for compound bow and the Open for recurve bow include athletes who can shoot standing, in a chair or with help to maintain balance, as long as they do not need to make any adaptations to the bow.

Wheelchair athletes whose disability requires them to make modifications to the bow, whether compound or recurve, compete in W1. When it comes to individual games, the best in five sleeves of three arrows wins; while, in teams, they have 24 launches.

Many archers with physical disabilities are reaching very high competitive levels. It is because this sport allows to develop sharpness, concentration, strength and precision, among other skills. Therefore, it is not surprising that archery has become a sport that is not only enjoyed by professionals, but is also a successful recreational activity.

6.3 Archery as a recreational sport

Archery today is a sport that consists of hitting as close as possible to the center of a target to obtain the maximum number of points. So far, there are seven modalities in archery as a recreational sport:

- Target archery
- Archery in the room
- Field archery
- Clout archery

- Run archery
- Ski archery
- 2D and 3D archery

These categories are explained in more detail below.

6.3.1 Target archery

The target archery is often ruled by the International Archery Federation or FITA (Féderation Internationale de Tir à l'Arc), which also regulates the Olympic rules.

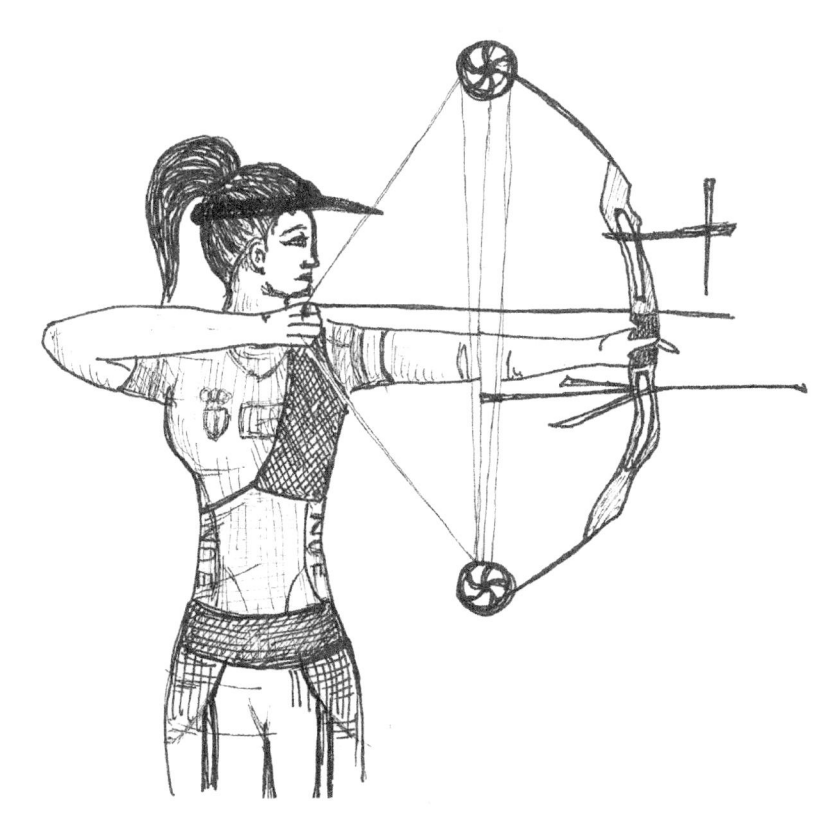

Archer in the compound bow modality

In these competitions, the targets can be both indoors, where the distances are between 18 and 25 meters, and outdoors, where the distances vary between 30 and 90 meters. The competitions are divided into three and six arrow finals, where archers have a limited time to shoot their arrows at targets divided into concentric circles. Each ring marks a score from 1 to 10, with the center of the target being the circle with the highest score. In outdoor archery targets, the central circle also has a small circle inside, called X, which is used to break the tie. Archers score each finish by adding the points from each arrow. The arrows that are touching a line have the highest score; in case of a tie, the archer with the higher number of X wins.

For each round, and depending on the distances, different types of target are used. These vary from 40 cm in diameter for a distance of 18 meters, indoors; 80 cm in diameter at distances of 30 and 50 meters; 122 cm in diameter in shots of 60 and 70 meters for women, and 70 and 90 meters for men, outdoors. These standards are regulated by the FITA, and they are the same as those used in Olympic competitions.

6.3.2 Field archery

Field archery is an outdoor modality in which archers shoot, in often uneven terrain, at targets located at different distances, although sometimes these are unknown.

The rules regarding distances, the type of target and whether or not the distances are known before the shot vary between different national and international associations. For this reason, there are competitions with distances known in advance, and others unknown, with maximums that vary, with targets that represent concentric circles and others that represent animals... In this sense, it is the modality that most resembles bowhunting, where it is also necessary to calculate distances in unknown environments, you have to fight the fatigue of having to walk on rough terrain, etc.

In terms of associations, the most important federation at a world level is the International Field Archery Association or IFAA, although the FITA and other institutions also have their own regulations regarding field archery.

6.3.3 2D and 3D animal archery

Archer practicing 3D modality

Within the possibilities offered by archery, the one that has most followers lately is undoubtedly the 2D and 3D animal archery. This shooting modality originated in the United States, although a short time later it passed to France, from where it arrived in Spain.

The easiest way to explain forest archery is to imagine a golf course, swapping the grass for trees, the holes for targets, and the golf clubs and balls for bows and arrows. There are two modalities in the forest archery:

- **2D**: it is the pioneer modality in the forest route. In this modality, the targets (21 in total) are photographs or drawings of animals placed on a parapet or support. Twenty-one targets are used in two dimensions. They have two scoring zones: the vital zone and the rest of the animal.
- **3D**: it is the most widely accepted modality today due to the great attraction of 3D targets. Volumetric pieces are used as targets; in other words, real-scale reproductions of animals made of derivatives of plastic, foam, etc., but with great realism. According to the World Archery Competition regulations, the targets will be arranged along a course, at distances unknown in advance, and which can be shot from different planes: up, down, with different angles and positions. The targets have three scoring zones: the inner vital zone, the rest of the vital zone, and the rest of the animal.

Depending on the type of bow and arrows used, there are five types of forest archery:

- ACO - Compound Bow
- ARE - Recurve Bow
- ARI - Instinctive Arch
- ALO - Longbow
- ADE - Bare Arch

The archers are distributed in groups (patrols) of 3 or 4 members and they solve the targets they find on their way. The tours will be 3 or 4, each different form the other, depending on the number of participants. The circuit must be duly marked with colored stripes and some direction arrows to indicate the path that the archers must follow after writing down their scores on the cards and collecting the arrows from the target. A group archer is the patrol leader, and they are responsible for respecting the rules and shooting order.

Since February 1, 2014, the Royal Spanish Archery Federation (RFTA) has modified the forest route archery regulations to adapt to the international regulations of World Archery, formerly FITA. Changes affected how shots are scored, target distances and silhouette type based on the size of your hit zone and how far away you need to be (minimum shooting distance of 5 meters, 45 meters for the compound bow and 30 meters for the rest of the bows) and at the disposal of the archer in the peg (shooting area), among others.

First of all, archers must know where to shoot from at different points along the route. Although the pegs for the 2D and 3D traversal are the same color, they do not indicate the same thing. As shown in the table below, in the 2D path the pegs seem to indicate the position from which the archers have to shoot; in the 3D tour, the pegs are also used to indicate the type of arrow that the archers have to use.

Pegs for the tour	2D route	3D route
White numbered peg.	The first one we found, where the patrol waits.	The first one we found, where the patrol waits.
Yellow peg.	Archer starting point.	Archer starting point.
Violet peg.	It is the timekeeper's station (if there is one) and where the archers who have shot wait.	It is the timekeeper's station (if there is one) and where the archers who have shot wait.
Blue peg.	Where the first shot is fired for every archer, generally the one with the longest distance to the target.	From where the two arrows are shot with a naked bow, instinctive recurve and longbow.
Red peg.	Where the second shot is fired for every archer, generally the one with the shortest distance to the target.	From where the two arrows are shot with a free or compound bow.
White peg.	From where children shoot.	From where children shoot, a maximum of 25 meters.

Specifically, the 3D targets are divided into groups based on the size of the 10/11/8 circles. These groups will indicate the minimum and maximum distances at which said target can be placed for the red peg (composite) and the blue peg (naked, instinctive recurve and longbow).

	Group 1	**Group 2**	**Group 3**	**Group 4**
Size of the 11/10/8	Size of the 11/10/8	Size of the 11/10/8	150-200 mm	<150 mm
Distance form the red peg	35-45 m	20-36 m	10-27 m	5-18 m
White numbered peg	20-30 m	15-25 m	10-20 m	3-10 m

There are also rules that establish the way in which archers must position themselves and shoot, both in 2D and 3D archery. More concretely:

- Archers will shoot from each side of the peg.
- Archers can be standing or kneeling.
- All archers shoot in pairs.
- Each archer has a maximum time of one minute to shoot, from the exit of the yellow peg to the release of the second arrow (in this time they can use the binoculars).

In both the 2D and 3D courses, participants shoot two arrows at each target, for a total of 24 in both types (48 shots in total). The following table shows how the score varies depending on the first and second arrows (since the first arrow is usually shot at a greater distance from the target) and depending on the area of the animal that the arrows pass through.

	2D route		3D route	
	Zone	**Total points**	**Zone**	**Total points**
White numbered peg.	Vital zone.	20	Internal circle of the vital zone.	10
	Wounded zone.	15	Vital zone.	8
			Rest of the animal.	5
White numbered peg.	Vital zone.	15	Internal circle of the vital zone.	8
	Wounded zone.	10	Vital zone.	6
			Rest of the animal.	3
Maximum punctuation.		**735**		**360**

However, there can always be arrows that end between two scoring zones or on the edge of the scoring zone. When this occurs, the arrow will always grope to the highest value:

- 11 points, the small circle in the center of the ring of 10.
- 10 points, the largest circle within the vital zone.
- 8 points, the vital zone outside the ring of 10 (lung).

- 5 points, the rest of the animal.
- The horns, hooves and areas of the target that are not animals (base, grass, trunk, stone) are counted as null.

The RFTA also establishes a series of general considerations so that the routes, whether for leisure or due to some competition, take place in the safest, fairest and most equitable way possible:

- All arrows used by an archer must be the same.
- All arrows must be marked with the archer's name and club.
- Broadheads will never be used on the courses, only ogival or combo.
- Camouflage or camouflage clothing will not be used, the archers must be clearly visible for their safety.
- In the event of an accidental release of an arrow, it will not be considered fired if the archer can touch it with his bow and without losing contact with the peg.
- The distance of the targets will not be discussed with the rest of the patrol.

This type of archery is one of the most popular today, since it combines elements of field and hunting archery. However, it is by no means the only one. There are even modalities that, despite being less known among fans and the general public, also have international competitions.

6.3.4 Clout archery

Clout archery can be practiced with any type of bow. This modality is very similar to target shooting, except that, in this case, the archer tries to hit a target on the ground at 180 yards (165 m) for men, and 140 yards (128 m) for women; for youngsters, and depending on age, there are also shorter shooting distances.

Target is marked by a 12-inch (30 cm) flag on a stake driven into the ground, with the flag as close to the ground as possible and practical. Usually six arrows are shot in each series of clout, up to a total of

36. A match usually consists of a double clout of two series of 36 arrows, which can be shot in the same or opposite directions (one round is thrown and returned to the starting point or the second round is fired from the flag of the first).

The winner will be the person who gets the most points. The score is measured with a rope with knots that mark the concentric scoring zones based on the distance they have been from the flag. The markings are gold (5 points), red (4), blue (3), black (2), and white (1). The rope makes a complete turn around the stake and, each time an arrow is found, it is placed in a marked area for each score. As with the target shooting, once all the arrows have been collected, the judges count the points out loud, starting with the arrows with the lowest score.

6.3.5 Flight archery

Flight archery can be done whenever there is enough space, as it happens in aerodromes or other large and fenced facilities. In this modality, the archers compete to see who achieves a greater flight distance. Although there are various modalities, as a general rule it involves shooting six arrows in different directions. Later, the archer goes to look for them and marks the arrow that has gone the furthest, while the judges measure the distance that the arrow has traveled.

Evidently, results vary depending on the type of bow used, the power... However, the key is to have an optimized bow kit. To achieve this, many improvements have been developed in the bow, something that has had a positive impact on the discipline of archery in general. The most obvious improvement is, perhaps, the recently developed carbon arrows, much lighter than other materials.

6.3.6 Ski archery

This sport is similar to biathlon, a winter sport that combines skiing with rifle shooting. In the archery modality, on the other hand, instead of a carbine, a recurve bow is used.

The track is established in the middle of the field, and the athletes slide it down on their skis while shooting at 16 cm diameter targets at a distance of 18 meters. There are two positions in which the archer can shoot: kneeling and standing. Regardless of the position chosen, the skis must not be removed at any time; only if the athlete wants to shoot while kneeling can the ski be untied, but they must remain in contact with it at all times. The circuit is 150 meters long and, in some competitions, the athlete has to complete a penalty lap for each missed target.

What this variety of forms that archery takes as a recreational sport demonstrates is that people always find a way to adapt this discipline to the circumstances. What was historically a tool for hunting and combat has become a hobby with great health benefits and also an elite sport. But, as expected, archery has not lost its traditional functionality, and today it is still used for hunting.

6.4 Archery nowadays

Archery hunting is the use of archery to kill animals. The difference with traditional hunting is the type of weapon used and, therefore, the effective range, which is less in the case of archery. Hunting with traditional type materials is much more challenging, since the use of modern equipment such as bows with pulleys with sight allows to increase the precision, the clearance, the penetration and, therefore, the effectiveness of the bow.

This modality of hunting with a bow is regulated in the same way that hunting with other weapons, sometimes with more or different restrictions or limitations than hunting with firearms. In fact, bowhunting is prohibited in several European countries: Germany, Ireland and the United Kingdom. There are two types of bowhunting: bowfishing and field or bush hunting.

6.4.1 Bowfishing

Bowfishing is a technique that consists of launching an arrow from the fishing post to a place where we see a bank of fish. The arrow is attached by a line to a spool located on the bow itself; after throwing it, it can be picked up without problems. If a specimen has been hunted, it will depend on our aim.

A WALK THROUGH ITS HISTORY

Bowfishing

Bowfishing is a technique which originated in the United States, where it is seen as a very popular sport, especially among young people looking for alternative forms of fun. However, bowfishing is nothing new since, as we have seen in previous chapters, Native Americans, both in the north and south of the continent, used this tool to bring food home every day.

The bows used are generally very simple. Most do not have a peephole, although some of them incorporate a long-range LED flashlight to see in the dark of night. Most of the bows are light, since less weight makes them easier to use, something that the archer appreciates after having made several shots. Two types of bows are mainly used for bowfishing.

- Traditional bows.
- Modern compound bows, which use a pulley system to assist the archer, and can have up to 50 pounds of draw.

Bowfishing arrows are considerably heavier and sturdier than those used with other types of archery. They are typically constructed of five to sixteen-inch fiberglass, but materials such as aluminum, carbon fiber, and carbon fiber reinforced fiberglass are also used for strength. However, these arrows usually lack fletching, the feathers that arrows used on land usually have aim to give them greater stability in flight; nevertheless, in the water, it can cause the arrow to change direction, and they are not necessary or useful at the relatively short distances associated with fishing.

The fishing line is attached to the arrow by tying it to a hole in the shaft of the arrow or by using a slip system. This line is often made from braided nylon. The resistance or weight of the lines range from 80 to 400 pounds (35 to 180 kg), or up to 600 pounds (275 kg) in the case of hunting alligators, a very common practice in the southern United States. Line color is typically lime green, white, or neon orange.

The fundamental thing of this modality is the aim. Throws are made at a distance of several meters, from a ground post (such as a rock) or a boat. Special attention must be paid to the refraction of the water, since it tends to distort the location of the fish, and therefore cause failure to hit the target. The actual compensation for the refracted light must be taken into account not only for distance and depth, but also for the angle at which the arrow must be shot.

Aiming below the target compensates for this optical illusion. The depth and distance from the animal also influence the direction in which the arrow should be aimed for the shot. To compensate for the distortion effect of objects in the water, aim 10 cm down for every 3 meters away from your target. As always happens, both in traditional fishing and in traditional archery, practice will help to improve the calculation of optimal measurements and distances to have a correct shot and increase the possibility of hitting. As for species, the most commonly hunted in freshwater include common carp, grass carp, big-head carp, crocodiles and paddlefish; in salt water, rays and sharks are commonly hunted.

It is true that the refractions caused by the water make bowfishing a particularly complicated modality. However, the terrestrial modality (that is, field or mountain hunting) also has its difficulties. Even so, this has not prevented the number of people who want to learn this activity from increasing.

6.4.2 Field hunting

No gunpowder, no shotgun. Little by little, hunting returns to the bow and arrows: it is the latest trend in the hunting sector, which is looking for a more sustainable and selective model, but also to attract a new public that wants to experience the most ancient and primitive sensations. According to Ángel López Maraver, President of the Royal Spanish Hunting Federation (RFEC), bowhunting is a model that has more and more followers. The organization calculates that there are a thousand people who practice bow hunting, plus another ten thousand foreigners who hunt in Spain every year.

There are different types of bow for this type of hunting. Generally, traditional bows are used: these are the simplest in design and are normally made of laminated wood and synthetic materials, and they are the ones that everyone knows from movies and/or literature. It is not usual for them to have aiming targets, so the hunter must coordinate sight, muscles and memory as the only reference. This concept is known as instinctive shooting. Basically, it's about shooting the arrow in the direction you're looking, focus, and shoot. It sounds simple, but mastering this form of shooting requires constant training. These types of bows allow for very fast shots, which makes them ideal for fly hunting, small game hunting, and hook or whip hunting.

However, compared to compound bows, they have less performance, since the energy that the bow is capable of transmitting to the arrow is less. This failure must be overcome by using heavier arrows with fixed blade tips that penetrate the prey more easily. The objective of the arrow is to bring down the animal quickly so that it suffers as little as possible. The degree of success is marked by:

- Precision: it is essential that the arrow hits some vital area of the prey. For this, it is better to use light arrows, which have a flatter flight and allow a greater degree of error in estimating a distance without resulting in a significant deviation in the point of impact.
- Penetration capacity: the arrow must have enough energy to reach the vital organs of the piece, going through hair and skin, and sometimes ribs or other bones. The heavier the arrow, the greater its penetrating power.

As we can see, there is a conflict between grazing (the maximum distance achievable with a tight shot, without significant fall of the arrow) and penetration. For the first factor, a light arrow is better; for the second, a heavy one. For this reason, you have to look for the arrows that adapt to the type of game or species that you want to shoot down. But, as with rifles, it is difficult to have an ideal bullet for all situations and for all game species. Of course, it also depends on the type of bow used to shoot the arrows.

Within the traditional bows, archers have the option of using the longbow or English bow, which is lighter and more manageable. The most modern ones are built by interspersing sheets of wood with other materials such as carbon or fiberglass. They are usually long bows of more than 65", and there are one-piece or detachable models on the market. The longbow's power curve is progressive and increases as the bow is drawn, making it suitable for both large and small games.

The same materials used to build the longbow (plywood, fiberglass or carbon) are used to build recurve bows, which fall under the category of traditional bows. Unlike the longbow, which is basically a flexible stick, recurve bows usually have a well-differentiated body from the blades, which are responsible for bending and doing the work. Its main feature is the double curvature of its blades, which improves performance.

Generally, the recurve bow is shorter than longbows, but with a larger grip and thicker limbs, making it heavier but more stable. In the market we can find detachable and one-piece models, it is even possible to have the same bow body with several blades of different powers and lengths to adapt the bow to the different needs that the archer may have. In recurve bows, the accuracy and power/speed ratio is better than in longbows, which is why it is usually the most widespread option within traditional bows. As for the longbows, they are valid for any type of hunting.

The tube or shaft of the arrows is made of the same materials as the bows, and there are even shafts that combine two of these three materials: wood, carbon or aluminum. At the end of the shaft, the feathers are placed, which, as we already know, help to stabilize the flight of the arrows. The feathers used in bowhunting can be natural or plastic.

The main drawback of fletching made from natural feathers is that they tend to make more noise when they rub against anything, including the archer's face at anchor, and they also get damaged in bad weather conditions, such as rain. On the other hand, they have the great advantage of recovering their shape immediately after being folded by rubbing against the bow window. However, plastic pens are more rigid, but they are also more resistant and durable. In addition, they can be used with arrow rests, which release the shaft when the archer releases the arrow and prevents friction. Therefore, they are the most used today and the standard option for those who hunt with pulley bows.

Pulley bows are responsible for the recent popularity of archery. These compound bows have pulleys at the end of their limbs activated by a system of cables. Thanks to these pulleys, the tensioning force necessary to keep the bow open is reduced. Unlike traditional or simple bows, and regardless of the size of the shooter, compound bows have a maximum draw. When this maximum is reached, the pulleys generate a «relaxation» effect that allows the bow to be held effortlessly and thus the archer can calmly aim at his target.

Pulley bows have an added sight and trigger that works like a trigger. Thus, the pulley bow is more like a two-armed drone than Robin Hood's weapon. Thanks to them, bowhunting has become accessible to many more people, since its use does not require as many hours of training as traditional bows and its performance and precision are much higher.

The arrow shot from a pulley bow travels at 100 m/s and is shot 30 meters from the target. There are two types of broadheads, those with fixed blades and those with mechanical blades; and there are arrows with two, three, four or even more blades. The normal thing, however, is to use arrowheads with two or three blades, since the greater the number of blades, the less the penetration of the arrow.

Two-bladed knives make a flat cut that penetrates the prey better, but also causes a wound that can be closed more easily; those with three leaves or more make a star-shaped cut that tends to open, which helps bleeding and finding the trail.

More recently, mechanical arrowheads have been developed, tips that remain hidden and attached to the body of the point, and only open when they hit the animal. This type of arrow has gained popularity in recent years, since its flight is perfect: thanks to its shape, they fly just like training feathers, and they can be designed with large diameters without fear of the length of the blades affecting the flight. A larger cutting diameter produces larger wounds, greatly increasing the lethality of this type of arrowhead.

These advances have not been without controversy. Environmental and animal groups have criticized that it is a cruel method that rarely kills the animal. For their part, hunters argue that the method not only does not stress the animal (the arrow is silent), but the blade points hardly cause them pain because they produce a very clean cut of the tissues. However, it is true that the current legislation has loopholes that sometimes lead to requirements from the authorities to the archers. To avoid this, the RFEC has asked the Central Arms and Explosives Intervention to create an «archer hunter card».

As a hobby, archery hunting requires no gun permit and no minimum age. Therefore, more and more women and children start the activity. It is not just about hunting or carrying out a pest control. According to data from the Ministry of the Environment, hunting reports a flow of close to 4000 million euros per year and 55 000 direct and indirect jobs. For this reason, hunting options without prey have multiplied, such as show dog competitions, compak sporting (a type of clay pigeon shooting that simulates the movements of partridges, quails or rabbits practiced by between ten and fifteen thousand people in Spain), or hunting in 3D, which we already saw in the previous section.

These activities are helping to make hunting known, something that Spanish hunters hope will translate into greater respect for this sport and for the hunting tradition. They allege that in countries like

Sweden or Finland it has become normal, and people go hunting to stock up on meat before winter.

Throughout the different chapters we have seen that, indeed, archery and its uses and traditions vary between countries and cultures. However, something that all cultures share and that has not changed throughout history is the symbolism of archery. We have already discussed, for example, the ritual character of the bow and arrow in Japan. In the next chapter we will go further and explore how the bow is present in all religious traditions. Also, we will see that archery is not only religion, but it is also science. And health![41]

41.- Sources reviewed for this chapter:
www.lograrco.es/
www.paralimpicos.es/
findeoutdoor.wordpress.com/
arcospa.wordpress.com/
trofeocaza.com/cazawonke.com/
cazawonke.com

CHAPTER VII
THE BOW AND ARROW: HUMANISM AND SCIENCE

Throughout the different chapters, we have seen how the precision, patience and autonomy that the bow and arrow provide have made them not only a reference weapon for different people throughout history and in different continents, but also a sport that attracts a growing number of followers. In addition to its historical and warlike significance, archery has also developed an inherently symbolic meaning, as a tool that extends the power of the body, becoming an extension of it.

Since the beginning of time, arrows have been a symbol of direction. It was not yet inherently associated with the bow, as it is today, but as one of the first pieces of technology developed by man and one of the easiest to understand, it was an essential part of communication between our ancestors.

It is said that, for the first Native American cultures, the arrows were part of a complex system of non-verbal communication. For example, two horizontal arrows in different directions could mean war, while a broken arrow meant peace. The crossed arrows were a symbol of friendship.

Having a pointed end and a feathered one meant movement. This directional characteristic of the arrow has been maintained throughout the centuries, and it has even been used to explain complicated scientific theories.

Arrows are also part of the modern world. In fact, they are an essential part of the urban landscape, where they are responsible for marking roads and paths. If it weren't for them, millions of people every day would be unable to reach their destinations. On the keyboard of our computers, in the microwave, or in any other scenario in which concepts as basic as «up and down» need to be transmitted, «right and left» or «forward or backward», our best ally is always an arrow.

For this reason, the arrow and the bow have been present in all aspects of human history, from the cruelest battles to current literary works, passing through great works of the Renaissance. The same characteristics that attract thousands of people to this sport today, have been used throughout the centuries as a symbol of heroism and power, a kind of extension of the body's power. Mastery of the bow and arrow was as impressive then as it is now, but it was also, more importantly for ancient tales, inherently spiritual.

In this chapter we will explore this aspect of archery. From the mythology of the oldest civilizations to the Abrahamic religions, the bow and arrow have served to explain concepts related to the human and the divine. However, they are not simply an esoteric and mystical symbol. Its symbolism is both so simple and so universal that it can be applied in all areas of human existence, including modern science.

How is it possible that such a seemingly rudimentary tool as the bow and arrow has anything to do with modern science? Read on to find out!

7.1 The bow: a mythological tool

Every February 14, millions of people celebrate Valentine's Day. This celebration, a tradition exported from Anglo-Saxon countries to the rest of the world, is usually associated with love, and it is not for nothing that the date is known as Valentine's Day. But falling in love is not the only form of love. For this reason, in countries such as Finland or Estonia, Valentine's Day is a tribute to friendship and it is called Sobrapäev and YstävänPaiva, respectively. In Bolivia and Colombia, the Day of Love and Friendship is celebrated, and it is celebrated in September.

Be that as it may, and whatever form of love is celebrated, Valentine's Day is associated with Cupid, a plump, blond, angelic-faced cherub who, with his arrows, is capable of causing infatuation. However, few wonder how Cupid, which has its origin in Roman mythology and is, therefore, pagan, is associated with Saint Valentine, a saint of the Catholic church. Moreover, there are many who believe that, since Valentine's Day is a day in which lovers and friends show their affection with gifts, the origin of the festival is merely commercial. But it's not like that; like many of the traditions we have today, we only have to look back to understand how little by little we have been incorporating elements and customs of our ancestors into our lives.

As we will see in this section, the bow and arrows have played a fundamental role in the mythology for different people. From ancient Rome and ancient Greece, to the Nordic and Asian people, this tool has helped to explain ethereal concepts such as love in all its variants, or trust and self-esteem, as well as natural phenomena, such as the seasons of the year or storms.

7.1.1 Cupid and Eros: the bow in Greek and Roman mythology. The origin of Valentine

Cupid has transcended as an icon of love in popular culture. He appears as a naked young man, with wings and arrows, who is sometimes blindfolded, as a way of representing the infatuation that arises without choosing oneself and from which perhaps the phrase «love is blind» comes. This bandage on the eyes also refers to the loving passion that prevents seeing the defects and evils of the loved one. The influence of Christianity has caused him to be thought of as an angel but, in his origin, Cupid was actually a Greek and Roman deity.

Cupid

In ancient Greece, the god responsible for sexual attraction, love and sex, as well as fertility, was Eros. His Roman equivalent was Cupid (desire), also known as Amor. In addition to being the god of love, he was responsible for the creation and order of all things in the cosmos, which could be related to giving the impulse inspiring to nature, which was always expanding.

The origins of Eros vary depending on the source consulted. On the one hand, legend has it that Eros was the son of Aphrodite, goddess of love (called Venus in Roman mythology) and Ares, god of war (known as Mars to the Romans); in some myths he was the son of Nicte and Erebo. According to Plato's Banquet dialogue, Eros was conceived by Poros (abundance) and Penia (poverty) on Aphrodite's birthday. It is enough to understand the origins of Eros to comprehend that the different stories represent the different aspects of love.

For Zeus the arrival of Eros was not a good prediction. The god of gods, knowing the arts of seduction and trickery of Eros, was convinced that his birth would bring catastrophe and chaos. Therefore, he ordered Aphrodite to get rid of the newborn. Far from following the instructions, the goddess hid her offspring in the forest, where the wild beasts nursed and cared for him. Thus, he grew up beautiful like his mother, wild like the beasts that raised him, and cunning and clever like his father.

When he grew up, Eros made himself a bow out of maple wood and some arrows out of cypress wood, and trained himself shooting animals. With practice, he developed masterful shooting ability and amazing aim. Realizing this, his mother gave him a bow and arrows of gold and lead. These had a gift: if he shot the golden arrows he granted love, but with the lead ones, he caused forgetfulness and hatred. Neither gods nor mortals were immune to the arrows of Eros. And, just like in real life, love is not always reciprocated.

The same thing happened to Apollo, god of light and the sun, and also of archery. While Cupid was practicing with the bow, the sun god humiliated him. Angry, Cupid followed Apollo through the forest until he ran into Daphne, a nymph. As revenge, Cupid shot one of his golden arrows at Apollo, and one of his lead arrows at Daphne. Apollo, in love with her, began to pursue a Daphne invaded by hatred and repulsion towards the god, ready to conquer her at all costs. In her flight, Daphne came to the Peneus River, where she asked her father, god of the rivers, for help. Taking pity on her daughter, he turned her into a laurel tree so that Apollo would stop persecuting her. A 17th-century sculpture by the sculptor Bernini captures the very moment when Apollo finally catches up with her beloved: Daphne is taking root, her hair turning into leaves. Apollo, affected, takes a couple of branches with leaves and places them on his head, with the intention of turning those laurel leaves into the symbol that he would represent them from that moment on.

Aware of his power, Eros sometimes refused the requests of his mother and the other gods to interfere in the course of the lives of some mortals, which caused more than one headache to the gods.

The more time passed, the more worried his mother was. She, in search of an answer to her son's behavior, went to the Oracle of Themis.

«Love cannot grow without passion», it told her.

Aphrodite did not understand these words until her son Anteros, god of passion, was born. Only when he was with his brother did Eros transform into a beautiful young man; when they parted, he reverted to the blindfolded boy. That is to say, love ceases to be blind at the moment in which passion also appears.

But how does a god from classical mythology relate to a Catholic saint? The answer is found in the Roman Empire, in the year 270 A.D. That year, Emperor Marcus Aurelius Flavius prohibited soldiers of the Empire from marrying, considering that married men were bad warriors. Valentin de Terna, then Bishop of Interamna (Terni), not only opposed this measure, but also invited young lovers to come to him for a secret marriage. Upon learning of this, the emperor summoned Valentin, who continued to refuse to obey orders despite being threatened with death, and even tried to convert the emperor to Christianity.

On February 14 of 270 Bishop Valentine was beaten, stoned and finally beheaded. Legend has it that while the bishop was awaiting the completion of his sentence, he fell in love with the daughter of his jailer, a blind girl. Thanks to her faith, Valentin miraculously restored her sight. Faced with his imminent execution, the bishop wanted to say goodbye to his girlfriend, and left her a message that he signed: «From your Valentine». In February of 380, Christianity became the official religion of the Roman Empire, but the pagan symbols did not entirely disappear. In fact, there are theories that the saints of the Catholic church are a legacy of Roman polytheism. Thus, in 498, when Pope Gelasius instituted the feast of Saint Valentine, considering him the patron saint of lovers, it is not surprising that the image of Cupid, considered the god of love, was associated with the festivity.

But, in addition to understanding love, the bow and arrow have been used to explain other aspects of human life. Different people throughout history have used deities to try to understand phenomena and events greater than themselves.

7.1.2 Archery in universal mythology

We started this book talking about the caves of Altamira, about those cave paintings in which our ancestors already appeared shooting arrows at some hairy bison. The figures, even being simple sticks, give us an idea of what the scene would be like in real life, and we can even imagine the direction in which the arrows were directed. These drawings were made hundreds of centuries ago, and many people throughout history have wondered why these images were drawn. A common explanation is that they represented something magical, a kind of ritual through which, even without having a concept of the existence of a god, the daily activities of the first men (hunting, agriculture) were expected to be favorably carried out for them.

Arrows in art are timeless. In fact, the cave paintings of the Iberian Peninsula and the rest of Europe are not the only representations of archers. As humans evolved, arrows became an adornment of other divine beings as well, and even a metaphorical tool in the stories that people have told themselves throughout history.

7.1.2.1 Greek mythology

Greek mythology has seeded our cultural heritage with countless myths and legends about many characters that are part of history today. An example of these myths are the famous Amazons.

Everything related to this tribe of warrior women is shrouded in mystery and legend, including its origin. Even scholars do not agree on where they lived: while some scholars believe that they come from the Caucasus area, others believe that they came from the left bank of the Danube, and others think that they originate from Sticia. This to name just a few places that are linked to its mysterious origin.

What is clear about the Amazons is that they were a people made up solely of female warriors. Legend has it that, to prevent any man from being part of their ranks (although the highest ranking Amazons had servants), they only had sexual relations with foreign males and, if they had male offspring, the children

were killed or terribly mutilated. If girls were born, the situation did not change much either, since their destiny was to have one of their breasts cut off; in fact, *mazon* means «chest» in Greek and *a* translates to «without»: no chest. This mutilation, however, had a purpose, even if it was only of a warlike nature, since it was practiced so that they could better handle the spear and, above all, the fetish weapon of the Amazons: the bow and arrow.

It should also be noted that, as part of this culture of femininity, the Amazons only worshiped the goddess Artemis, the Hellenic goddess of wild animals, virgin land, births, virginity and maidens, who brought and relieved women's diseases. According to the legend, it was the goddess's way of life that guided these formidable warriors, leading them to the greatest victories. It is said that they even fought against Athens, after Theseus took the goddess Antiope to her land. They are also credited with founding the city of Ephesus and building the great Temple of Artemis.

Among the most famous Amazon warriors that have gone down in the annals of history is Penthesilea, who, despite being killed in battle by Achilles, showed her bravery and her worth in combat during the Trojan War, comparable to the wildest. Also noteworthy is Hippolyta, sister of Penthesilea, who possessed a magical belt that gave her certain powers on the battlefield.

But, in addition to the classical tradition, the bow and arrow also appears as a symbol of gods and mythological creatures from other traditions, from the Nordic countries to countries in the Far East.

7.1.2.2 Nordic mythology

«Ullrheitireinn, sonrSifjar, stjúpsonrÞórs. Hannerbogmaðrsvágóðr ok skíðfœrrsvá at engimáviðhannkeppask. Hann er ok fagrálitum ok hefirhermannsatgervi. Á hanner ok gott at heita í einvígi».

Edda Prosaica, SnurrySturluson.

> Ull, son of Sif and adopted son of Thór. He is such a good archer and ski racer that no one can rival him. He is beautiful to look at and has all the makings of a warrior. It is also good to call him in duels.
>
> Edda Prosaica, SnurrySturluson

Unlike what happens in other mythologies, the Nordic gods are not part of a complex system of characterizations and hierarchies, but rather are divided into two great races: the Æsir (gods) and *ásynjur* (goddesses) who come from Asgard (the Nordic equivalent of the Greek Olympus) and who perform functions of government and war; and the Vanir, inhabitants of Vanaheim, to whom fertility functions are attributed. Each of the gods was a member of an assembly, headed by Odin, supreme god of all the Nordic gods; and god of wisdom, death and war. But, in addition, he was the father of many of the gods.

Among those gods was Thor, god of thunder. Thor, in turn, was married to Sif, goddess of wheat and fertility, and adopted her son, **Ull (translated as power), god of winter, also known as the god of hunting, of the archery, winter sports and death.**

Ull had an extraordinary ability to chase his prey through the woods without the snow being an obstacle to reaching his goal. He possessed a bone in which he had engraved magical formulas, a bone so powerful that legend has it that it even allowed him to cross the frozen sea riding on it. He was known for his skills as a hunter and would roam the Ydalir (yew forest) mountains, searching for his prey using special shoes (what we now call skis). **Being the god of hunting and archery, among the symbols that represent the god are a quiver full of arrows and a large wooden bow.** On occasions, he appears near a yew tree, the tree whose wood he used to build his bow, and the same wood European archers traditionally used to build their tools.

But, in addition, Ull played an important role in explaining the seasons of the year. Legend has it that, as a punishment for having deceived a young woman, Odin was expelled from Asgard for long periods. During that time, Ull was in charge of ruling the Nordic Olympus. It was then that winter came to those lands.

7.1.2.3 Asian mythology

In previous chapters we have talked about the bow in the Asian continent, and how countries like China, Japan, Mongolia and Brunei share this ancient tradition, each with its variants, which have also been an inspiration for each other. It was in Asia that the horse archer first attained mystical symbolic power, and the first continent where the arrow became an object of importance and ritual, a source of power.

The bow and arrow in Hinduism and Buddhism

Before acquiring its ritual character, as in Japan, **the arrows were used for magic practices. Belomancy, a form of divination using arrows, is very popular in Asia: eleven arrows are put in a sack and, depending on where they point when drawn, the omens of the gods can be interpreted.** In Tibet, belomancy is based on a slightly different method, called Ge Sarmda'mo, after the semi-mythical King Gesar. Numbered arrows are placed in a container and shaken until one falls out. The number would correspond to an entry in a divination book.

These types of divination are still carried out in northwestern India today. One of these age-old games is *teer*, which consists of betting on how many arrows, shot by professional archers, hit a rotating barrel-shaped target. And it is that arrows are a very popular element in Hinduism, especially in *Ramayana*, one of the great epics of Hinduism (the other is *Mahabharata*). Written in Sanskrit, its nearly 50 000 verses are divided into seven books. Its writing, dated 2400 years ago, is attributed to the Hindu sage Valmiki, whose arguments and multiple secondary stories and adventures have been a literary inspiration throughout the centuries.

Ramayana recounts the adventures of Rama, one of the incarnations of Vishnu (the protector), who is considered a divine human, a mortal god who personifies and explores the ideal characteristics of the person. In one of his exploits, Rama defeated the demon King Ravana using the so-called Arrow of Brahma, which had feathers of winds and points of sun and flame. Like so many legends, this story was also metaphorical, and from Rama we inherit the phrase «one arrow, one word», which implies the goal of integrity and infallibility.

However, the most famous archer in Hinduism is Arjuna, a central character in the *Mahabharata*, an epic that overshadows great classics such as *The iliad* or *The odyssey* in length and scope. Arjuna is so famous that there is an annual award in India by that name, which is given to Olympians who have excelled at the international level and have shown special abilities in leadership and discipline.

In *Mahabharata*, Arjuna receives as a divine gift a magical golden bow, Gandiva, and two *caraj* that never run out of arrows. According to legend, every time Gandiva shot it made the same noise as thunder, and the power of it was so enormous that the bow had to be returned to the gods. Experts speculate that, in the world of the poem, the bow is actually a metaphor for confidence and self-esteem: with both characteristics, just as armed with a bow and arrow, a person can achieve anything they set their minds to. Archery is itself an allusion to the path of inner exploration that every human being must undertake in order to develop their character.

Arrows are also present in other Hindu ceremonies. In a boy-naming ceremony, known as *KaJerKaThoh*, a bow and three arrows are placed in front of the baby, each carrying a great deal of symbolism. The first arrow refers to the land, the second to the clan and the third to the newborn. Tradition dictates that the bow should be kept in a safe place throughout life, since when its owner dies it will be placed next to the body, once the three arrows have been shot into the sky, signaling that they will accompany the soul of the deceased on its journey to the afterlife.

This symbolism of the bow and arrow is also found in the Buddhism practiced in northern India, Nepal, Bhutan and Mongolia. The decorated arrows, called *dha*, are part of the Buddhist shamanic culture, and these are part of the art, mythology and theological tradition of the region. They are considered sacred weapons, held by the gods and praised in sacred texts. Mongolian shamans even sew arrows into their clothes; their rattle is supposed to drive away demons.

It should be noted that, in eastern Mongolia, bow and arrows are part of marriage rituals. Traditionally, the father of the bride presents the groom with arrows and a *caraj*, before the bride and groom are joined in marriage. Next, the father delivers an ode to the arrow, detailing qualities that are expected to reflect the characteristics of its new owner (the groom). In short, the arrow becomes a symbol of the groom's status as the new head of the family, thereby granting him permission to act in its defense.

This symbolism of archery is not unique to Buddhism. In Eastern Asia, more specifically in China and Japan, there is also evidence that the bow and arrow serve to explain not only theological aspects, but also aspects inherent to the human being.

The bow and arrow in Eastern Asia

As we have seen, there is a great tradition of archery in Asia. In Chapter 4 of this book we already explored how the Japanese tradition spoke of the skills of the samurai Nasu no Yoichi, who became a Buddhist monk and remains a popular figure in Japan, where they do not forget his great feat: knocking down a fan placed in the top of a post on an enemy ship, thus achieving victory for the Minamoto clan. The mythological part states that Yoichi killed a demon with his sacred bow, a ritual that continues to this day in the Shinto and Buddhist traditions of Japan.

We have also talked about the tradition of archery in China.

The first thing we narrated was that, more than 2000 years ago, Yang Youji became the first archer in ancient China. But, even before Yang Youji was born, **and even before Confucianism, Buddhism and Taoism were mixed and gave rise to the great Shinto cultural richness, Chinese mythology already narrated the exploits of HouYoi, also known as Shenyi or simply Yi ( ), the god of archery.**

> He is sometimes depicted as an archery god descended from heaven to help mankind. In Chinese mythology, the sun is symbolized as a three-legged crow, called a sun bird. Legend has it that, at the beginning of time, there were ten of these suns, all of them

descendants of Di Jun, God of the Eastern Sky. The ten sunbirds resided in a mulberry tree in the Eastern Sea; each day one would travel around the world in a chariot driven by Xihe, Mother of the Suns. Finally, the birds got tired of the routine and decided that they should all go up at the same time. The heat from the land intensified: crops withered and lakes and ponds dried up. Humans and animals had to take refuge, those who did not die of exhaustion.

Time passed and the suffering continued. Emperor Yao decided to ask for divine intervention and plead with Di Jun for help. Di Jun was aware of the misdeeds and sent Houyi, the god of archery, to teach his sons a lesson, asking him to scare them into killing him, so they wouldn't act bad again. Houyi also wanted to end the crisis peacefully, but a single glimpse of the scorched earth was enough to convince him that drastic measures were necessary. Enraged at the people's suffering caused by the sunbirds' misconduct, Houyi raised his bow and shot them one by one. Upon killing the ninth, Emperor Yao was quick to stop him, as killing the last would leave the world in total darkness. Houyi accepted and was hailed as the hero of humanity, but his actions made enemies for him in Heaven and as a result he was punished with divine wrath. As a father, Di Jun could not forgive Yi, so he decided to punish him by expelling the hero from the heavens and stripping him of his immortality. He thought that, if Houyi cared so little for mortals, he should live like one. So Houyi undertook a series of epic adventures to save China, much like the adventures Odysseus had during his return to Ithaca. Although Houyi cared little about being expelled from Heaven, he could not bear to think that one day he would die and cease to exist. Seeking a way to regain immortality from him, he traveled to the palace of Xi Wang Mu, the Queen Mother of the West, on Kunlun Mountain, seeking an elixir of immortality. The goddess knew of his deeds and took pity on him, she gave him the elixir, but on one condition: knowing that Houyi was a skilled architect, she asked him to build her a summer palace in exchange for immortality. He accepted and worked for many months. Before leaving, Xi Wang Mu warned Houyi that the two elixirs she had given him were the last of their kind. Houyi planned to use it on himself and his wife, Chang'e.

However, Houyi's wife passed away before she could take it. The pain of losing his wife completely changed him: he became violent and went from being a hero welcomed by mortals to being hated as a tyrant. So much so that his disciple, Feng Meng, beat him to death. Although Fen Meng was brought to justice, Houyi met a bitter end due to his high-handedness. However, when he died, his spirit ascended to the sun and he built a palace that he lived in with his wife. Thus, Chang'e and Houyi ended up representing *yin* and *yang*, the moon and the sun.[42]

Today, this mythology is part of the Chinese cultural tradition. **Archery has a tradition in polytheistic religions such as Buddhism and Taoism, but the three monotheistic religions (Judaism, Christianity and Islam) also include archery in their narratives, both in a real and metaphorical sense.**

7.2 The bow in Abrahamic religions

In the middle of the year of the Hebrew calendar, Jewish boys and girls go out to play with bows and arrows. The bow symbolizes a rainbow; and the arrow, the power of inwardness, a mystical part of the kabbalistic tradition. What is celebrated within the Jewish tradition, the first monotheistic tradition in history, is Lag Ba'omer, the day the plague ceased among the disciples of the famous Rabbi (teacher) Akiva, as well as the anniversary of the passing of Rabbi Shimon bar Yochai, a rabbi who lived in Galilee at the time of the Roman occupation.

But archery found its tradition already in the holy Jewish scriptures, in the Old Testament. In 798 B.C. reigned in Israel Joás, twelfth king of Israel, and third king of the dynasty of Jehu. Although he did not remove the golden calves that Jeroboam I had erected after the death of King Solomon and the division of Israel, Israelite tradition has it that he still followed the national religion of Israel. He goes on to say that when the prophet Elisha was on his deathbed, Joash went to see him. The prophet made him shoot an arrow in the direction of Syria and hit the ground; Joash agreed, but only did so three times. Therefore, El-

---

42.- Legend taken from: mitologia.fandom.com

isha told him that he alone would defeat the Syrian troops three times. The prophecy was fulfilled, and Joash defeated Ben-Hadad III's troops three times and sacked Damascus several times. This is how Joash recovered all the territories that his father, Jehoahaz, had lost.

Arrows are also part of the Islamic tradition. However, it is not true that, as popular legends claim, they are used as in Tibetan traditions as a form of fortune-telling. In fact, the techniques of witchcraft and magic are prohibited by Islam, either because they are associated with charlatanism and deceit, or because they are related to the *jinn*, the demons.

However, they are part of the Muslim apocalyptic narratives. For example, they are included as part of the iconography that represents the main signs that will occur shortly before the end of the world and the arrival of Judgment Day. More specifically, they are associated with Magog and his sovereign Gog, who represent the archetypal enemies of the chosen people and of God. The Qur'an describes that: «Gog and Magog will walk until they reach the mountain of Al-Jamar, and it is a mountain of Baitul Maqdis, and they will say: 'We have killed those on Earth. Now we are going to kill those in the sky', and they will shoot their arrows into the sky and the arrows will come back to them smeared with blood».

But, in addition, the prophet Mohammed himself used the arrows as a metaphor to talk about how extremists would misuse religion at the end of days, before the Last Judgment. In Sahih Bukhari, written by Mohamed Al-Bukhari and considered by Sunni Muslims to be one of the two most reliable collections of *hadiths* (narratives of the life of the prophet) together with Sahih Muslim, it is recorded:

«I heard the prophet say: "In the last days (of the world) there will appear some young people with absurd thoughts and ideas. They will speak well, but they will pierce through Islam like an arrow through a buck, and their faith will not go beyond their throat"».

Arrows are also mentioned in the Bible, around sixty times, and often as metaphors. One of the best known passages is the passage from Samuel 20:20, in which Jonathan helps David, who had fled from Naiot of Ramah. To find out what David should do, Jonathan shot three arrows:

«I will shoot three arrows towards that side, as if I were shooting at a target, and I will tell my servant: "Go get the arrows". If I tell him:

"The arrows are this way from you; go on, take them", you can leave calmly, because nothing is going to happen to you. I swear to the Lord. But if I tell you: "The arrows are beyond", go away, because the Lord wants you to go».

However, arrows are most present within the Catholic tradition in its iconography.

7.2.1 Arrows in religious art

Every August 26, the Carmelites celebrate the transverberation of Saint Teresa of Jesus, the first female doctor of the Church. The saint narrates this mystical experience, the one that led her to make a special vow to God and prompted her reforms, foundations and her path to holiness, in a poem called *My beloved for me*. Specifically, in her last stanza, she says:

> He hit me with an arrow
> Engorged with love
> And my soul was made
> One with its Creator.

Another famous woman related to the Church, although she was not religious, is Joan of Arc, also known as the Maid of Orleans, a young peasant woman considered a heroine in France for her role in the Hundred Years War, after having claimed to have visions that incited her to fight for Catholicism.

Her contemporaries recognized Joan as a heroine of the Loire Campaign. During the battle, the young girl was injured by an arrow that struck between her neck and shoulder while she was holding her banner in the trench in front of Les Tourelles. Regardless, she returned later to encourage the troops in a final assault that brought the surrender of the fortress. In 1430 Joan was captured by the English and accused of heresy, a crime for which she was punishable by death. But, in addition, Joan had fought in the war pretending to be a man, with which she was also convicted of transvestism. The punishment was the stake.

Joan of Arc

Several eyewitnesses described the scene of her death on May 30, 1431. Tied to a tall pillar in Rouen's Vieux-Marché square, she asked friars Martin Ladvenu and Isambart de la Pierre to hold a crucifix before her. Once dead, her remains were burned twice more to reduce them to ashes and prevent them from being collected as relics, and then they were thrown into the Seine River. Her executioner, Geoffroy Thérage, would later say that he «feared being cursed because he had burned a saint».

However, the quintessential saint when it comes to arrows is Saint Sebastian, a fervently Catholic man, born in Narbonne and raised in Milan. Although his beliefs did not align with military life, he traveled to Rome in order to enlist in the army so he could secretly help his co-religionists. He was appointed captain of the Praetorian Guard by Emperor Diocletian, and became one of the ruler's «favourites».

Saint Sebastian and art

When Saint Sebastian went to Rome, he was able to help many Christian prisoners, although he did it in secret, since at that time Christians were persecuted by the Romans. But Saint Sebastian had to be especially careful: when it is mentioned that he was the «favorite» of Diocletian, many experts say that, in reality, Saint Sebastian had a sentimental relationship with the emperor. When he found out about Sebastian's beliefs, he asked him to renounce them, but the saint refused.

Diocletian felt like a spurned lover, so he ordered Sebastian executed by shooting countless arrows at him. Saint Irene was in charge of going to collect the body of the martyr but, to her own surprise, Sebastian was still alive. Secretly, she took him to a place where he could heal. When he had recovered, far from wanting to escape from Rome, he publicly confronted the Emperor Diocletian, in a scene reminiscent of the confrontation between William Tell and the governor that we described in a previous chapter. The furious Roman emperor ordered Sebastian beaten to death and his body thrown into a sewer.

The body of the saint was taken from the sewers and buried in the Via Appia, in Rome. Little by little, devotion to the martyr turned him into an emblem of the subculture: cut off from society because of his beliefs and preferences, persecuted by an intolerant majority, but someone who survives and is able to face his persecutors. With this growing popularity of the saint, also came extensive iconographic representation. The oldest description dates back to the 5th century, and was found in the Roman crypt of Saint Cecilia, more specifically in the catacomb of Saint Callistus.

Throughout the centuries, artists have seen in Saint Sebastian a symbol of Hellenic beauty, as if it were the Christian Apollo. For this reason, different creators from different artistic disciplines have addressed the subject of this Catholic saint. In the world of literature, Oscar Wilde used his name as a pseudonym when writing after his release from prison; Walter Pater wrote Sebastian von Strock in 1886, in which he refers to the martyr as «a passive young man courting death». The martyr also appeared in texts by important writers such as Jean Cocteau, T. S. Eliot, Franz Kafka, Thomas Mann or Tennessee Williams. Already in the 20th century, painters such as Redon or Moreau, and photographers such as Holland Day, continued to use Saint Sebastian as an emblem of physical and erotic beauty and redemption from suffering.

Until the Middle Ages, Saint Sebastian was portrayed as a naked young man with a loincloth, with a contorted pose and pierced by arrows, generating a very dramatic scene. It could suggest «the epitome of sadomasochism» to many, which is why it became a subject of sexual myth. It was during the Renaissance that Saint Sebastian began to be a recurring theme in works by artists such as Botticelli, Tintoretto, Titian and El Greco, among others.

The arrow, as we have seen, is a literary, artistic and religious symbol. But, in the same way that it has been used throughout the centuries as a metaphor and allegory in the humanities, it has also served to explain scientific phenomena.

7.3 The bow and arrow in science

The arrow is a simple, but so universal symbol that it is applicable to all areas of human existence, including modern science. The first to use the concept of the arrow and to use it as a metaphor to explain scientific phenomena was the British astrophysicist Arthur Eddington (1882-1944), when he related the expression «the arrow of time» to the second law of thermodynamics, just as it is described in *The nature of the physical world*:

> [...] Let us arbitrarily draw an arrow. If by following the arrow we find that the proportion of the element of chance is increasing in the state of the world, then the arrow points to the future; instead,

when this proportion decreases, the arrow points to the past. [...] I will designate with the phrase «arrow of time» this characteristic of time without spatial correlative, which consists of having a way in a certain direction. In space, no analogous characteristic is found. [...]

Eddington's words highlight an important concept, the substantial difference between time and space. For example, if we can move in all directions in space, how is it possible that we cannot travel to the past and back? This approach is not new, since Aristotle asked himself the same question in classical Greece. More recently, noted scientist Stephen Hawking further developed the concept of the arrow of time in his popular book, *A brief history of time*.

According to the theoretical physicist and cosmologist, on a human scale, we can understand that time has a unique direction, and that this idea influences our perception of space-time and even expressions such as *yesterday* and *today*. However, at microscopic levels, this not only would not be true, but time could even be reversed. The «arrow of time» means that things will always tend towards entropy and disorder rather than concert, a theory that Hawking used to explain the (finite) expansion of the universe.

For those of us who are not theoretical physicists, or even scientists, this very philosophical explanation of the history of the universe can be a bit complicated. However, the explanation does reflect the usefulness of metaphors to explain complex ideas, and that, whatever technology is developed, arrows will always be part of the popular imagination.

On a more practical scientific level, more specifically in the field of medicine, archery is performing a beneficial function. A study carried out by the Infanta Leonor Hospital in Madrid in 2019 revealed that a project developed by the Mijas Hunters Society is changing the lives of many women whose breasts were removed due to cancer.

In its particular fight against the disease, the Mijas Hunters Society is determined to change many women's lives on a physical and psychological level; and, for this, it has partnered with Gran Arco, a store in Granada specializing in archery, and with a physical therapist.

In just one year of archery practice, a high percentage of women managed to recover enough mobility in their arms to be discharged and able to return to work.

According to a program instructor who works directly with these women, the vibration caused in the bow by the exit of the arrows is capable of improving lymphatic drainage, which helps them regain mobility and facilitates their return to normal life. We cannot think of a better application for these two simple and ancient objects.

In addition to a form of therapy, we have seen that the bow and arrow have also served as unbeatable weapons of war throughout history, as an identifying element of the gods, and as a metaphor for the origins of our universe. Therefore, it is not surprising that they have been fundamental elements in the great works of universal literature, and that their legacy endures to this day in works of fiction.

7.4 The bow and arrow in literature and fiction

The attraction of archery is indisputable: it combines skill and aim, as well as the possibility of practicing it outdoors. That is why it has been reflected in numerous works over time in any type of artistic medium: literature, painting, cinema, comics, sculpture. There are so many references to the bow and arrow in art that it would be enough information for a book that only covered that part. That is the reason why the following are just some examples.

The bow and arrow have appeared in the great works of literature since the dawn of time. The English have told the stories of the archer Robin Hood and the Austrians have recounted the exploits of William Tell. But, before this, great classics of universal literature, such as *The iliad* and *The odyssey*, already included archery in their lines, presenting it as a symbol of manhood, strength and power.

However, they have not been the only works. More than 2000 years after Odysseus returned to Ithaca, the famous German composer Richard Wagner was writing *The ring of the nibelung*, a cycle of four operas based on figures from German mythology written in the mid to late 19th century. A century later, and inspired by this opera, the

British philologist and writer J. R. R. Tolkien wrote the now famous trilogy of *The lord of the rings*, which in 2001 would become feature films by the filmmaker Peter Jackson. Epic novels had men as protagonists, but also other anthropomorphic cultures, such as hobbits, dwarves and elves.

Anyone who has seen any of the films remembers Legolas, the sindar elf, prince of Mirkwood, played by Orlando Bloom. Beyond his long platinum blonde hair, Legolas stands out as an avid archer. The scene of his arrival in Moria is unforgettable, when the Company of the Ring is attacked by the guardian of water, a creature similar to the Kraken, a kind of giant octopus from Nordic mythology. When Frodo, the hobbit protagonist of the trilogy, is about to be swallowed by the beast, Legolas manages to save him by shooting the guardian with an arrow in the eye. Once in Moria, Legolas demonstrates again his archery skills, slaying hordes of goblins and wounding a cave troll over and over again with his arrows. He only runs out of arrows once, at the Battle of Helm's Deep, after slaying numerous Uruk-hai, a superior race of orcs from Mordor.

However, Legolas is not the only archer in fiction. In 2008, the first installment of *The Hunger Games* was published, the first book in a trilogy of adventure and science fiction narrated in the first person from the perspective of Katniss Everdeen, a sixteen-year-old teenager who lives in Panem, a post-apocalyptic nation located in what was formerly North America. Panem is divided into twelve districts, and every year twelve boys and twelve girls are forced to participate in a reality show called «The Hunger Games». There is only one rule: kill or be killed.

The story begins when Katniss volunteers instead of her sister in those games that are so reminiscent of the Greek Olympics. The young woman already stands out as an archer. In her introduction, she shoots an arrow at an apple located in the mouth of a pig in the watchers' restricted area, stunning everyone. Thanks to her bow and arrow, she manages to survive the games. However, the legacy of her acting and her «irreverence» make her a threat to those in power, but an inspiration to the poor and downtrodden of Panem.

The hero and the antihero figures are very recurrent in literature and in other forms of narrative, such as comics. The debate about whether or not comics should be included as a form of literature is a separate debate, but for the purpose at hand it is enough to highlight the narrative function of this genre.

The bow and arrow are present in many vignettes as a representative weapon of some of the main characters. One of the most outstanding examples is the Marvel character, Hawkeye. Clint Barton and his brother were orphaned when his parents died in a car accident. He was only eight years old. Six years later, they ran away from the orphanage and high school to join a traveling carnival, where the swordsman, the carnival's star attraction, recognized Clint's talent for archery and began training him day and night. Thus was born Hawkeye, the shooter, who would end up as part of the Avengers.

Hawkeye is an excellent archer and an expert at designing and building new arrowheads. He has a special bow that allows him to shoot up to three arrows per turn, and he always carries 36 arrows and 36 different arrowheads in sheaths on his face; he can mount an arrow in two seconds. The arrowheads, however, are special: there are those with acid, others with cables that entangle and paralyze the enemy, electric, explosive, magnetic... whichever one Hawkeye uses, depending on the circumstances, it aims to complement the powers of his partners.

Another example is found in Green Arrow, a DC Comics character. Although billionaire Oliver Queen is often thought of as nothing more than a modern-day Robin Hood, Green Arrow is much more. Raised on cotton wool, Oliver Queen took all his privileges for granted until, by a tragic accident, he is stranded on a desert island. The situation of loneliness makes Queen seriously rethink his existence and he finds within himself all his strengths in order to survive and not to lose his head in the attempt. But, in addition, he takes advantage of time perfecting one of his skills, archery, and becomes the best archer the world has ever known.

When he manages to return to civilization, he decides to use his fortune and his unparalleled marksmanship to become a kind of urban vigilant, dedicated to cleaning the streets of his native Seattle and Star City of corruption and crime using his bow and arrow.

EPILOGUE

Perhaps this is the best way to close this book. We have talked about the bow as a tool for different people throughout history, but that prevalence reflected something else. Indeed, like the heroes of fiction and mythological stories, archery is a reflection of the best qualities of human beings. Perhaps it would be worth to write a long conclusion, even a separate chapter, to collect everything we have learned about archery through these pages. However, as happens so often, others have already found the perfect words to describe what we mean.

In our case, the famous writer and novelist Paulo Coelho perfectly describes the essence of archery, and what I hope to have conveyed throughout these pages. With his permission, I borrow his words:

> An action is a thought that manifests itself.
> A small gesture denounces us, so we have to perfect everything, think about the details, learn the technique in such a way that it becomes intuitive. Intuition has nothing to do with routine, but with a spiritual state that is beyond technique.
> Thus, after much practice, we no longer have to think about all the necessary movements, since these become part of our very existence. But for that, you have to train, repeat.
> And if that wasn't enough, you have to repeat and train... The arrow is the intention that is projected into space. Once it has been fired, there is nothing the archer can do, apart from following its path towards the target.
> From that moment on, the tension necessary for the shot no longer has a reason to be.
> Therefore, the archer keeps his eyes fixed on the flight of the arrow, but his heart rests, and he smiles.
> At this moment, if you have trained enough, if you have managed

to develop your instinct, if you have maintained elegance and concentration throughout the shooting process, you will feel the presence of the universe and you will see that your action was fair. and deserved.

The technique ensures that both hands are ready, that breathing is precise, that the eyes can be fixed on the target.

Instinct makes the moment of the shot perfect.

Whoever passes by and sees the archer with open arms, following the arrow with his eyes, will see that he is still. But the allies know that the mind of the person who fired the shot has changed dimensions, it is now in contact with the entire universe: it continues to work, learning all that was positive about that shot, correcting possible errors, accepting its qualities, waiting to see how the target reacts to being hit.

When the archer draws the string, he can see the whole world inside his bow. When he accompanies the flight of the arrow, this world approaches him, caresses him, and makes him have the perfect feeling of duty accomplished.

A warrior of light, after fulfilling his duty and transforming his intention into gesture, has nothing to fear: he has done what he should.

He has not allowed himself to be paralyzed by fear, and even if the arrow has not hit the target, he will have another chance, for he has not been a coward.

THE END

BIBLIOGRAPHY

CONSULTED SOURCES

imperioromanodexaviervalderas.blogspot.com/.../documento-de-flavi...egecio-renato.html
es.wikipedia.org/.../wiki/Batalla_de_las_Termópilas
es.wikipedia.org/.../wiki/Historia_de_la_ciencia
www.biblegateway.com/.../passage
es.wikipedia.org/.../wiki/Arco_compuesto
es.wikipedia.org/.../wiki/Escitas
es.wikipedia.org/.../wiki/Pueblos_escitas
es.wikipedia.org/.../wiki/Tiro_con_arco
es.wikipedia.org/.../wiki/Arco_y_flecha
es.wikipedia.org/.../wiki/Cultura_maya
es.wikipedia.org/.../wiki/Juana_de_Arco
es.wikipedia.org/.../wiki/Guerra_de_Vietnam
es.wikipedia.org/.../wiki/Imperio_incaico
www.lograrco.es/.../sumeria-3-500-a-c
www.lograrco.es/.../el-arco-y-las-guerras-medievales
www.lograrco.es/.../espana
www.lograrco.es/.../inglaterra
www.lograrco.es/.../mongolia
www.lograrco.es/.../japon-yumi
www.lograrco.es/.../indios-nativos
www.lograrco.es/.../recorrido-de-bosque-3d
recreacionhistoricachile.wordpress.com/.../la-sanidad-en-el-e...lman-y-la-arquería
www.actualidadliteratura.com/.../el-cantar-de-rolda...atalla-de-hastings
www.efemeridespedrobeltran.com/.../enrique-ganara.-ho...ique-de-trastamara
www.efemeridespedrobeltran.com/.../crecy.-hoy-26-de-a...-derrota-a-francia
historia.nationalgeographic.com.es/.../conquista-normanda_inglaterra_15697
www.abc.es/.../abci-batalla-aljub...-201308022002.html
www.artehistoria.com/.../video/batalla-de-crécy
arcohistorias.blogspot.com/.../11/un-poco-de-historia.html
www.timetoast.com/.../1750-1914-a4931b12...-8017-94777a642cac

www.chinatoday.com.cn/.../s2006n4/p42.html
lucerorodriguezg.wordpress.com/.../la-parabola-de-la-flecha-envenenada
books.openedition.org/.../cemca/4046
www.monografias.com/.../culturas-que-encontro-colon
www.ecured.cu/.../Civilización_incaica
tlanepa.blogspot.com/.../10/plebeyos-mayas.html
blog.aljaba.net/.../articulo-invitado-...n-el-tiro-con-arco
arcospa.wordpress.com/.../29/tipos-de-arcos
cazawonke.com/.../68490-los-nuevos-c...arco-y-las-flechas
www.trofeocaza.com/.../reportajes-caza-con-arco/tipos-de-arcos-para-caza
findeoutdoor.wordpress.com/.../11/bowfishing-o-la-pesca-con-arco
arcospa.wordpress.com/.../flechas
www.trofeocaza.com/.../tipos-de-flechas-y...aza-mayor-con-arco
fedecazacyl.es/.../los-nuevos-cazador...l-arco-las-flechas
www.abc.es/.../abci-nuevos-cazado...72114_noticia.
html pateandolimites.com/.../dpv-tiro-con-arco
www.paralimpicos.es/.../deportes-paralimpicos/tiro-con-arco
liderazgoymercadeo.co/.../el-camino-del-tiro-con-arco
mitologia.fandom.com/.../wiki/Houyi
www.elperiodico-digital.com/.../el-santo-que-fue-a...gay-de-la-historia
redhistoria.com/.../mitologia-griega-e...to-de-las-amazonas
marveldatabase.fandom.com/.../wiki/Ojo_de_Halcón
elredondelito.es/.../la-historia-de-cup...ido-y-san-valentin
www.penguinlibros.com/.../265442-los-juegos-...uegos-del-hambre-1
lenguajeepo155.blogspot.com/.../11/ramayana-y-mahabharata_8.html
trianarts.com/.../p-coelho-de-el-guerrero-de-la-luz
www.motivaciones.org/.../MOTIV001/ctose1203.htm
mitologia.fandom.com/.../wiki/Houyi
www.elperiodico-digital.com/.../el-santo-que-fue-a...gay-de-la-historia
www.uyanajacu.com.ar/.../historia-del-tiro-...imbolismo-cultural
www.uyanajacu.com.ar/.../tiro-con-arco-y-di...s-mitos-y-leyendas
redhistoria.com/.../mitologia-griega-e...to-de-las-amazonas
marveldatabase.fandom.com/.../wiki/Ojo_de_Halcón
www.adeprin.org/.../cual-es-la-historia-de-cupido
bibliotecadelatierramedia.fandom.com/.../wiki/Legolas
esdla.fandom.com/.../wiki/Legolas
sites.google.com/.../jakelinepinedaepica/el-ramayana-mahabharata

Printed in Dunstable, United Kingdom